# Votes of Confidence

*"Alyssa's book provides some terrific insights* to up your game and confidence level to help life throws at you. There are some real use... can use immediately and share with others (especially your kids). This book is a must read for anyone who is interested in any level of self-improvement for yourself or others!"*

Brad Neilley
Global Vice President/CHRO
**Pentax Medical**

*"When frequently asked to describe the traits of high performing business leaders, I highlight individuals who have extreme confidence expressed without ego or false bravado. Alyssa unveils an easy to follow and practical approach through the Personal Confidence Dashboard and Plan that allow anyone to enhance and build out this critical leadership skillset."*

Mike Dallas
Senior VP, Human Resources
**Hewlett-Packard Company**

*"Confidence is at the heart of an individual's success and an important attribute that organizations look for in their workforce. This impressive book explains how to build confidence and does so with clarity that everyone should read."*

Shakti Jauhar
VP, Global HR Operations & Shared Services
**PepsiCo**

*"Finally, scientifically-based content, and a user-friendly process, that give us the power and means to conquer 'what is holding us back'."*

Lawler Kang
Author, **"Passion at Work"**
Engagement Expert
Entrepreneurial Igniter

*"Working with both HR and education professionals, there is clearly an underlying belief that confidence is something that develops as a result of lifeline learning or luck. Alyssa's book proves otherwise - that confidence can be increased and controlled at any age, by anyone. My own success is due to the same principles as Alyssa points out and acted as a compass to helping me reach all of my goals. Thank you, Alyssa, for crystallizing what I have always somehow known, but could not put into words."*

Mark Fogel
CHRO
**Success Academy Charter Schools**
5-time National HR leadership & Innovation award winner
Human Capital Thought Leader

*"Everybody needs a little attitude adjustment and this book provides the kickass confirmation you need to succeed. What are you waiting for? This is a sign!"*

Jeffrey Hayzlett
Primetime TV & Radio Host, Speaker, Author
**Chairman C-Suite Network**

*"In a very likable style, Alyssa's book explains the social secrets and leading edge science about confidence so that anyone can quickly become a more confident, successful individual."*

Michele Tillis Lederman
Author, **"The 11 Laws of Likability"**
CEO, **Executive Essentials**

*"Kickass Confidence offers a prescriptive for impacting results by getting at the very core of one's own ability to succeed in all areas. Alyssa Dver has succeeded at providing clear actionable steps that without a doubt, will have a profound impact on anyone wishing to up their game and excel in business and in life."*

Alison Martin-Books
CEO
**Mentoring Women's Network**

*"Clearly there is a connection between mind and body that scientists are now beginning to explore. In addition to movement control, Alyssa explains how the practice of mindfulness can be an important tool to help anyone to control confidence."*

John Rothwell
Professor of Human Neurophysiology
**UCL Institute of Neurology**


*"In this amazing book, Alyssa explores the possibility of handling emotions - in particular individual confidence - as a controllable thinking and decision process to empower the neuroplastic mechanisms that are engaged during motor and cognitive function."*

Dr. Angelo Quartarone
Consultant Neurologist/Neurophysiologist
**University of Messina**, Italy
Adjunct Professor **at City College of NY** and **New York University**


*"Confidence is a complex and critical topic, too often addressed with sentiment and romance. It's great to see it tackled for once with sense, insight and appreciation of its complexity and power."*

Margaret Heffernan
Author, **"Willful Blindness", "A Bigger Prize"**
& **"Beyond Measure"**


*"Witty and insightful, Alyssa Dver reveals confidence with a fresh perspective, helping us instantaneously make better choices and up our game!"*

Lina Taylor
**Beach Volleyball Olympian 2000 & 2004**
Founder of **Mission SOAR**

*"Confidence is the key to personal success and Alyssa's insights shed light on the biggest challenge we all face. This book will help you in more ways than you can imagine."*

Bob Wilkie
former **NHL player, 2 time WHL All-Star,**
**& American Hockey League All-Star**
Founder, **I Got Mind**


*"Alyssa Dver has delivered the one-two punch in showing us not only what confidence can do for you, but how it helps you BE your best self. Practical, wise and at times humorous in its honesty, this book will get you where you need and want to go!"*

Janet Neal
Founder & Queen Bee at The Superbwoman, Inc.
Author, **"Soul in Control: Reflections of a Reformed Superwoman"**


*"Great coaching for the person you may need to help the most – yourself!"*

Marshall Goldsmith
New York Times bestselling author of **"Triggers"**, **"MOJO"**
and **"What Got You Here Won't Get You There"**
**Thinkers - 50 Top Ten Business Thinker &**
**Top Rated Executive Coach in the World**

*Kickass Confidence* books are available at special quantity discounts for corporations, not-for-profit organizations and academic use. Also available: Workshops, TED-style presentations, confidence coaching and coaching certifications.

## www.AlyssaDver.com

## www.AmericanConfidenceInstitute.com

info@AmericanConfidenceInstitute.com or 508.881.5664

Book design by Justin Reis

First edition
10 9 8 7 6 5 4 3 2 1

# Kickass Confidence

*Own Your Brain.*
*Up Your Game.*

**Alyssa Dver**

Mind Full Press
*a subsidiary of Z. Holden Publishing*

# Table of Contents

# Dedication

To Dr. Joaquin Farias

*– A man whose confidence and commitment proved to me just how much a single person can individually control and contribute*

**kick-ass**

*adjective*

1. having a strong effect on someone or something; forceful; powerful
2. exceptionally good; spectacular, impressive, etc.

Webster's New World College Dictionary Copyright: © 2010 by Wiley Publishing, Inc., Cleveland, Ohio.
Used by arrangement with John Wiley & Sons, Inc.

# Foreword

The universe kicked me in the head. After a concussive series of attention-getting, undeniable coincidences, I was confident it was some kind of life calling. It turned out to be a confidence calling.

Eight years ago, my now 15-year-old son Zak started having uncontrollable movements with both his arms. After seeing a dozen doctors and spending over a year searching for solutions, he was finally diagnosed with a neurological movement disorder called dystonia.

It is estimated that over 300,000 people in the US have some form of dystonia. Some dystonia patients have issues with only a subset of muscles (focal dystonia) that do not properly operate, as is the case with my Zak. Others have a more comprehensive lack of muscular control.

As a simplistic explanation, dystonia is caused by damaged neurological connections between the brain and some muscles. This subsequently causes uncontrolled movements that typically look like tremors or spasms in the affected areas. Even though Zak has a relatively mild case of dystonia, he is unable to do things that other people take for granted, such as writing, shaking hands, brushing his hair, or holding his hand over his heart to pledge allegiance. More severe cases make it impossible for the person to stand up straight or cause the body to be in complete and perpetual spasmodic activity.

Dystonia is caused by a variety of factors including genetic mutation, stress, reaction to medication, and other environmental factors that corrupt neurological function. Children, the elderly, musicians, dancers and singers are frequent sufferers, though dystonia knows no specific age or ethnicity. In fact, someone with dystonia can have symptoms that ebb and flow or even suddenly disappear and sometimes reappear. The Department of Defense is one of the biggest contributors to dystonia medical research because a significant proportion of returning traumatized soldiers become unexplainably dystonic.

Medical treatments range from oral medications to often painful botulinum neurotoxin injections (most commonly known as the brand Botox®), to surgically implanted electrical brain devices.

Dystonia isn't fatal, but it is in all forms, debilitating and, so far, incurable. Like most disabilities, it stomps on the confidence of patients and caregivers alike.

Disabilities bring with them social stigmas plus frustration, and even anger, at one's lack of luck and ability. It certainly hits the confidence of kids and adolescents beyond expected teenage angst.

As a parent, I continued to wonder what I did wrong in vitro or as a role model. I questioned both my and my husband's genetics. I also questioned my ability to cope with the situation and whether my other son, Ben, would also develop such a 'defect.'

In my quest to mitigate my son's disruptive symptoms, treatment discomfort and physiological side effects, I explored the areas of alternative medicine and mindfulness. I found that acupuncture, meditation, yoga and other techniques temporarily—at best—helped quiet the dissonance between mind and muscle.

For Zak, his calm comes from playing tennis. Tennis is one of the few sports he can play, and fortunately, he is very talented and still very much enjoys it. He plays competitively and thankfully finds a unique comfort on the court. Miraculously, his dystonia isn't apparent when he plays. Tennis enables him to be confident, concentrated and in control. I am still stunned by how aggressively whacking a tennis ball enables him to put his mind and body at peace.

Meanwhile, with my continuous professional pursuits as a marketing strategy advisor, I continue to explore how and why people perceive personal value. Since college, I've been a fan of motivational theories that try to explain and anticipate why someone does (or does not) take action. I'm a Maslow[1] groupie and I apply his hierarchy of needs to everything I do in life and at work. It makes me much more conscious of my own responses and those of others. It also makes me be very considerate when calling other people into action as we do routinely as managers and marketers.

Layered on this perspective, while I have worked with hundreds of companies and thousands of executives around the world, I am continually amazed at the obvious and common insecurities that dominate most people's behaviors—and often damage their careers and/or their companies.

Four years ago, I decided to probe further and ran a confidence-focused survey that became the basis of my 2011 book, *Ms. Informed: Wake Up Wisdom for Women*. *Ms. Informed* was a sassy look at women's confidence that prescribed lessons for better confidence, primarily focused on helping women to have more self and social awareness. The book received welcome responses from readers, including men who read it themselves before handing it to their wives, friends and sisters. I also found that older women were giving it to a daughter or niece with comments to me such as, "I wish I knew this when I was her age." My biggest fans came from HR professionals including my now American Confidence Institute (ACI) partner, Lynnette Rumble. Lynnette and other

HR experts encouraged me to take the concepts of *Ms. Informed* and make a version that was more gender-neutral and corporate-friendly.

Beyond the supportive encouragement Lynnette gave me, she also taught me about the applied technologies and techniques being used by elite athletes. Lynnette's specialty is providing life coaching to professional and Olympic athletes as they transition from active sport to "real life". She exposed me to the surprising amount of insecurity these athletes experience as they try to figure out how to carry on life without their athletic entourage or identity. What we realized during these discussions was that these athletes had in fact, learned how to be confident in their respective sport worlds and subsequently, they were being taught again how to be confident in their new "life" roles.

Together we delved further by researching tools, technologies and techniques being used to help the athletes focus so they would avoid distraction and reach desired goals. This led us to learn about how neuroplasticity factored into their training and was enabling them to get into the now well-recognized state of mindfulness commonly called "the zone"...just like I had seen Zak do so many times on the tennis court.

That's when I realized the universe was calling me and insisting that I kick myself into gear and focus on this divine connection of brain and body. I read dozens of neuroscience research reports and pored over numerous books and videos on the topic. I learned the neuroplasticity vernacular and research so that I could have substantive conversations with 30+ neurologists, psychologists and executive coaches from around the world. My own mind became filled with science and stories about people being cured and conditioned using a variety of techniques that induced neuroplasticity. The culmination of all that karma, curiosity and content is compiled in this book.

Even though there is much more scientific research to be done, it is clear to me that the concepts of mindfulness (Eastern) and medicine (Western) are finally coming together in a provable, practical way that makes alternative medicine more mainstream. Every neurologist that I spoke to said neuroplasticity is real and 'may' be a significant compliment, and in some cases, a legitimate alternative, to available medicines and medical devices. Moreover, corporations and individuals are recognizing the importance of wellness, mindfulness and self-awareness to improve employee engagement and productivity—let alone lower medical costs and absenteeism. Popular media headlines the benefits of mindfulness and "owning your brain" to increase memory, concentration and longevity. From Goldie Hawn's MindUP classroom programs[2], to Lumosity's popular memory exercise app[3], there is little doubt that we can proactively change our brains to think and perform better.

Meanwhile, in our harried worlds, we juggle multiple life roles while being perpetually poked with messages about what we should know or do. We all struggle to arm ourselves with calm thoughts, consistent control and bulletproof confidence to support even everyday decisions. Fortunately, neuroplasticity can help here too – by consciously changing the brain physically to consistently think and act more confidently. Therefore, it is time to bring this simple, but very powerful, confidence conditioning to the masses. I fundamentally believe that anyone can become more—actually kickass— confident.

With this goal, Lynnette and I established ACI to continue finding and doing social-scientific, confidence research— synergizing the work of neuroscientists, psychologists and life/executive/business coaches. ACI's mission is to make available easy-to-use tools and information that help anyone assess and increase core confidence in themselves and in others.

We have seen awe-inspiring results. You'll read in this book about how high performance athletes use these techniques to improve their focus and control so they can be more effective on and off the field. We have worked with businesspeople who increased their confidence and impact by making difficult decisions clearly guided by their confidence to know with certainty that they were doing the right thing following their values.

We have even witnessed Zak be visibly healed using painless and quick neuroplasticity movement therapy so that he can now shake a hand, write and do what everyone typically can. With this clear evidence, not only did Zak's capability increase, his confidence soared. I even watched as my Parkinson's tremoring stepfather used the same techniques to grab control of his muscles by proactively mastering his own mind.

As I saw these measurable mental and unarguable movement-controlling miracles with my own eyes, I knew that I found a calling—to help others own their brains, up their games and live as confidently as possible.

Understanding what confidence is and how it impacts everything we do will fundamentally change the way you see yourself and others. You will learn that our greatest gift to ourselves and to others is our neuroplastic 'presence'—the ability to be mentally tuned into our own brains so that we can control our resulting behaviors.

I hope that with new and improved confidence, you will achieve great career and leadership success. I hope your new confidence will give you the ability to appreciate where you are in life, who you've become, and the confidence to get to where you want to be. May you also exude impactful charisma that encourages others to also be their best.

By increasing your confidence, you will reduce stress by learning to let things roll off your back more easily. Additionally, you will more often opt to take the high road by realizing your confidence isn't determined by anything or anyone else.

And my highest aspirations: may the knowledge you gain from these pages let you laugh a little louder, love a little more patiently and gracefully inspire others by practicing simple acts of confidence.

> *"Somehow I can't believe that there are any heights that can't be scaled by a man who knows the secrets of making dreams come true. This special secret, it seems to me, can be summarized in four Cs. They are curiosity, confidence, courage, and constancy, and the greatest of all is confidence. When you believe in a thing, believe in it all the way, implicitly and unquestionably."*
>
> Walt Disney

# Intro

Walk into a bathroom at the Cambridge Innovation Center (CIC) and you'll see dozens of MIT and other brainy entrepreneurs incubating transformational businesses. Among the buzz of shared espresso makers and high speed personal and fiber networks, you'll find old-fashioned paper flyers taped in the restroom stalls advertising meditation, yoga and other relaxing mindfulness classes. Apparently even brilliance needs to be "relieved."

Today, corporate wellness programs are in full throttle as they seek to reduce the stress and sickness caused by our over-informed and extreme-expectation workplaces. Executive coaches and work-life balance initiatives are put in place as deliberate speed bumps to help frenetic employees stop, think and connect to their minds—a luxury that is sadly sacrificed by 24/7 digital connectedness.

I fundamentally believe that despite access to information and people, digital connectedness is creating a new kind of loneliness and ignorance. It is easy to fall for social media staged standards that promote what everyone else seems to be doing, wearing or knowing. The base assumption reinforces that everyone else is better and the ease of unfiltered, bidirectional conversation makes it easy to confirm that—sometimes to a point of cyberbullying or worse. As businesspeople, we often measure relationships by the number of transactions, and we plan them in scripts we call user experiences. We often forget that trust and time are critical human and consumer needs which are not always predictable or programmable.

Therefore, I worry most about future generations. Children learn confidence from their environments and on top of digital social pressures, global demands subject American children to escalating academic standards together with and an imposed scaffolding of constant extracurricular stimulus. For the past two decades, we have been positively parenting children by telling them they can do anything—and that everything they do is just wonderful. Only now, at the expense of raising the most insecure generation, we know that building superficial self-esteem can come at the expense of mastering resilience and appreciating the lessons of failure.

> *"Success is the ability to go from failure to failure  without losing your enthusiasm."*
>
> Winston  Churchill

The constant social and economic pressure most of us experience costs us a lack of self-control. Regretfully, we all yell at someone we care about or do something that jeopardizes a relationship, job or perhaps our safety.  But slowing down isn't really an option. If CIC needs to catch its residents literally "mid-flow" in the restroom, it's all too telling that it's not usually practical to take a "mind-flow" break.

Our society's modern mantra is "You aren't doing enough." Meditate more. Eat better. Exercise more. Be present. Be more productive. Push yourself. Grow. Connect.  "Do cool Sh*t"[4] or "Just Do It®"[5]—whatever "it" includes.

This book offers a way to help manage all of this stress and subsequent guilt, without adding a lot of time or effort to your already overwhelmed life. *Kickass Confidence* will unmask what confidence is, as well as what it is not. We will then gently explore the science of confidence from neuroscience and psychology perspectives as well as the tools used in executive, life and business coaching. You'll learn about the latest research and theories that indicate anyone can physically change his or her own brain structure and function.

While trying to keep this a short and easy read for busy people who are not scientists, I want to give you enough of the science to give you immediate confidence in my premise that you can quickly and sustainably develop more confidence. Feel free to skip that section if you really just want to know how to do it. At the end of the book, we'll discuss the process developed at ACI that can help anyone quickly increase confidence, maintain it over time and incidentally pay it forward by becoming a role model for other people so they too become more confident.

In the book, *The Confidence Code*, Katty Kay and Claire Shipman[6] note, "Success correlates more closely with confidence than it does with competence." Clearly, confidence is the key to unlocking the potential in us and if you also believe, in the spiritually guided universe. It is also the key to effective leadership because it gives a leader both a figurative and literal sense of presence—a calm, controlled mind that appreciates the current moment and subsequently projects innate charisma and authority.

Like physical training, building core confidence helps push our limits further and in return, gives us more resilience to overcome obstacles. Like a personal coach within ourselves, confidence propels us forward to our desired destination. Confidence isn't a supplemental vitamin but rather an actual source of energy/chakra/qi that powers our competence.

Elite athletes know this. Many professional and Olympic athletes do emotional training using technology to help them quantitatively and predictably get to and stay in a confident "zone" aka "flow" (isn't it funny how is all comes back to the bathroom?) Ah heck, while we have that "stream" of thought, confidence conditioning is like doing Kegels[7] with your brain!

All it takes is about 15 minutes to start and thereafter, a few moments per day to proactively reflect. You also will need an openness to change your view of yourself and others. Lastly, the process requires you to have the courage to adjust your attitude and behavior to be different and ultimately be inspiring.

> *"Excellence is not a singular act, but a habit. You are what you repeatedly do."*
>
> Aristotle
> (& Shaquille O'Neal)

# The Ultimate Asset

You can go to a top college, have an impressive job title and/or have lots of money—but none of this means you will have confidence. I will argue that those competitive achievements and expectations could, in fact, increase temporary self-esteem while reducing sustainable confidence. I bet you know many people who are more pretentious than confident about their accomplishments and possessions.

I once made the mistake of saying to a group of elite athletes that the rest of us envied their confidence on and off the court. The athletes aggressively corrected me and said that their confidence was largely staged. Since very young, they had been taught how to act on the field and in front of media. They said that in all other aspects of their lives, they were actually VERY insecure, as their comfort was limited within and around their sport. Playing the learned role of athlete, they could be situationally confident as a means of achieving peak performance—as well as a way to intimidate competitors.

> *"If you don't have confidence, you'll always find a way not to win."*
>
> Carl Lewis

No doubt, you have experienced being around someone that actually is not that handsome or beautiful, not athletic and not otherwise obviously endowed. Yet, he or she beams with an unapologetic confidence that is viscerally attractive. Those people are "sexy and they know it"[8] and everyone else subsequently thinks so, too.

Some celebrities consistently appear confident such as: George Clooney, Angelina Jolie, Sean Connery, Bill Clinton, Morgan Freeman, Bono, Sting, Mick Jagger, etc. These people all project unwavering confidence—they don't seem to let anything ruffle their feathers. Whether this is all part of their public persona or who they are in reality, most of us are not privy to know.

> *"It's not how good you look.*
> *It's about how good you think you look."*
>
> *Andy Warhol*

However, if we were actually able to get a glimpse into the celebrities' private lives (like when I was able to talk directly to the elite athletes), we would undoubtedly find out that the celebrities have confidence issues, too. Despite being trained public performers who are meticulously managed to project a specific image, a celebrity's confidence also ebbs and flows. Just ask someone who lost on Oscar night or whose troubled love life is on display at every supermarket checkout.

So the great news for all of us is that no one's confidence is consistent or comprehensive. Everyone has areas they feel good about and other areas, not so much. The better news is that confidence isn't inherited or determined by nurturing. While parenting and childhood experiences can contribute to confidence, it is now scientifically evident that anyone can build more confidence—no matter what your upbringing or current circumstance.

Again I quote from the book, *The Confidence Code*, by Kay and Shipman[6]. This compendium of confidence research concludes, *"Confidence is something we can, to a significant extent, control. We can all make a decision at any point in our lives, to create more of it."*

To that point, let's go back and understand how athletes proactively learn how to be confident. There is a well-known performance phenomena referred to as "being in the zone" or "having flow." Athletes have long appreciated the state where body and mind are so connected at a moment in time that they can accomplish unimaginable feats such as shooting dozens of successful free throws or sprinting in the last few miles of a marathon. When athletes are in the zone, they report that time slows down and they are literally in the moment and able to exercise total mind/body control. They are not distracted by external noise; nor do they have doubts about their own abilities. They can therefore execute above and beyond what is "normal."

It is an athlete's Holy Grail to be able to intentionally get into and stay in the zone on demand. To achieve this, high performance athletes do three different types of training:

1. **Skills training**: This is the basic ability or competency to play their sport at an elite level. This includes all forms of physical training to increase stamina and decrease reaction time. It also includes the ability to handle any equipment needed to play the sport.

2. **Mental training**: Athletes learn how to alter their play depending on the specific conditions (i.e. type of court, altitude, weather, etc.). They also consider the specific opponent, and will adjust strategies for that game based on each other's strengths and weaknesses.

3. **Emotional training**: Top athletes also learn how to identify and remove any emotional issues that may distract or cloud their concentration. Even if something is subconsciously tucked away, it may still create enough distraction to lessen the athlete's performance. Sports psychologists and other professionals work with athletes to deal with any such potential thoughts before they hijack the athlete's intended game.

As we'll discuss in the chapter, "The Science of Confidence," some athletes take their training to an even higher level and use technology to help them reach and sustain zone or peak performance. Just as they build their strength and muscle memory, they aim to build neurological strength to enable their brains to filter and concentrate on their goals (literally and figuratively)! By using assisting technology, the athletes can simulate and measure confident thoughts that over time become mental memory paths and eventually autonomic responses. Precision-performance military are also using similar techniques and technology. Think about a sharpshooter maintaining focus despite being in a warzone or otherwise stressful environment.

So what can we take away from this concept of emotional training into our regular, non-athletic, non-sharpshooting lives?

You can train for a specific profession and be really good at that type of work. You can even study the competition and hone your game to be the most qualified. However, if you allow emotional distractions into your work and life, it will inevitably impact you performance and results.

For example, in the past you may have had to prepare a presentation on information that you were confidently an expert. You practiced the slides to a point of memorization and you even arrived at the venue in advance to ensure all the equipment was working perfectly. Then, with a yawn from someone in the audience, a momentary remembrance of a morning fight with your spouse, or a sudden panic that you may have some lunch stuck in your teeth, such distractions may have derailed your performance. Those are all legitimate concerns. However, if you are truly in the zone, those thoughts won't even enter your mind. When you are in the zone, you are completely focused on the task and feel ultimately confident in your ability to deliver the desired results.

> *"Peak performance has also been defined as a state of superior functioning whose characteristics are clearly focused attention, lack of concern with outcome, effortless performance, perception of time slowing down, and a feeling of supreme confidence."*
>
> "Peak performance and the perils of retrospective introspection."
> Brewer, Van Raalte, Linder, & Van Raalte, 1991. [9]

However, you can't remain in the zone all the time. It's really a purposeful, temporary state needed for high performance activities. So while back flipping off a balance beam may not be in your daily routine, you may have an important meeting or need to focus on a challenging project. These tasks require high performance—so can doing a presentation, having dinner with your in-laws or being on a first date. Anytime you require ultimate control of your behavior and emotions, I consider that a high performance situation.

We can, therefore, use the theories and techniques to build everyday confidence to better control and cope—no matter what life has or will kick you with.

# Confidence Defined

Ask ten people and you'll get ten different definitions of confidence. LinkedIn groups and bloggers create forums for people to comment on how much confidence they have overall and more specifically, what types of things make them feel confident. At the American Confidence Institute (ACI), we've seen and heard thousands of perspectives. There are many ways people raise their confidence, from getting a salary increase to wearing high heels!

Confidence is also a broad term that is used in many different professional fields and spaces of human interaction. For example, an entire field deals with the intricacies of the stock market and consumer confidence. Macroeconomic models and survey instruments calibrate the buying confidence of a mix of individual consumers in their wiliness to buy and sell things. This is then extrapolated to determine a measure of how healthy the economy is. In statistics, confidence can be calculated by confidence intervals that tell us "give or take a specific amount of doubt, we believe this is accurate." There is even confidence between people that translates to interpersonal trust—we confide in people by sharing "confidences" or telling one another something "in confidence."

The kind of confidence we are talking about in this book is often referred to as self-confidence. However, at ACI we don't like the term "self" since we fundamentally believe that part of ultimate confidence is making an altruistic contribution to other people's confidence. That is, confident people are role models, mentors and teachers and they inherently, as well as intentionally, impact the confidence of other people. Thus, it might be better for us to call the type of confidence we will address in the book "human-confidence" but that's not verbally sexy or inherently intriguing. As a marketer, I owe you the confidence that investing time and money to buy and read a non-fiction book must give you something of value—something that isn't intuitively obvious or otherwise old news. I also realize that we all actually do judge a book by its cover and title!

There is also some social taboo about the subject of confidence. If the book was just titled, "Confidence," you might not want to read it or have the gumption to recommend it to someone else. Like sexual dysfunction (and yes, that's another confidence topic!), it's not easy to admit publicly that we all could use more confidence. Most ironically, it takes strong confidence to admit that you aren't confident!

It's also hard to educate others about confidence unless you are confident. Like the cobbler who does not wear enviable shoes, you don't want to be taught how to be confident by someone that is not. And the truth is, truly confident people are few and far between. For me, it took five decades, tribes of people and an abundance of resources to be able to write and speak confidently about confidence. The key for me was learning to be confident enough to appreciate that I am not always nor all together confident!

It also helps to know about other people's "not confident" behavioral traps and projected attitudes. It helps us to be better-prepared to deal with those personalities and stay strong so they can't push us off our own confident tracks. And, while it heightens sympathy, it also becomes somewhat humorous to witness other people's bonehead, insecure behavior.

With all of this considered, we still need a definition of the kind of confidence we are discussing here. After collecting, brewing and tinkering with the recipe, ACI finally landed on a well-cooked definition that we feel is digestible, accurate and applicable.

> *CONFIDENCE is being certain of and acting in accordance with your own values and beliefs.*

This definition requires that you have clarity about what is important to you, and that you live by those priorities. It also implies that you do it despite what other people are doing or thinking. You are certain about your values and you let those values guide your actions despite potential consequences. You don't have to be a freedom fighter but you at least stand up for yourself and what you want to do and say.

However, we also know this may not be practical given the bumps and bruises life brings. We know that sometimes there are obstacles in terms of other people, circumstances and things that you just can't control. As a result, the team at ACI decided to extend the confidence definition. Once again we looked to sports and physical fitness for a metaphor to describe mental fitness.

> *CORE CONFIDENCE is having the inner strength to uphold those values - no matter the circumstance - allowing you to always perform at your best.*

As core training is fundamental to being physically strong, so it is to being mentally confident and resilient. Core strength strengthens the entire body. Arms and legs can do more and sustain stress longer. Core strength helps us avoid injury and allows us to rebound faster. Women with strong core muscles recover from childbirth faster. People with back pain often find core training alleviates, if not removes, their aches and helps them do more—including workout. Core strength helps us sit up taller and subsequently reduce physical conditions that then are treated with occupational therapy and/or medical intervention. Therefore, the concept of core strength transfers perfectly to the definition of confidence in that basic confidence is a sureness of who and what you are.

Core confidence is the additional ability to maintain that sureness no matter what life throws you. While you may get derailed due to a work or relationship issue, core confidence helps you get back on track faster and ideally, with less effort. With well-conditioned core confidence, you are prepared with a mental martial art that protects and empowers your performance.

> *"Confidence...thrives on honesty, on honor, on the sacredness of obligations, on faithful protection and on unselfish performance."*
>
> Franklin D. Roosevelt

Developing a six-pack of core confidence doesn't require sweat or starvation. It is enabled with maturity but can be accelerated with the right information, tools and practices. Core confidence helps you muster through challenges and always be mindful about who you want to be and how you want to be known. Core confidence isn't about sucker punching someone else, but rather knowing how to control yourself in light of other people's issues. It's a method to gain self–awareness as well as learn how to quickly deal with other people without having to memorize anyone's Myers-Briggs[10] acronym or PI[11] score. Conscious confidence is Eastern mindfulness meets Western medicine all combined into a meaningful and modern-world package. It is a way for you to take on the world in a graceful, productive way that protects you and the people you want to help. With core confidence, you will feel and look stronger physically and mentally and have a presence inside and out. Most importantly, you will be able to stay in control without pills, shrinks or any heavy lifting.

# The Look of Confidence

Walk into a bar and just look around. You can make immediate judgments about who is confident and who is not—just from looking at them. It is a combination of how straight they stand, the eye contact they make with others, how much they fidget or twirl their hair, and generally a reflection of what they are wearing or doing.

Now think about someone you know personally that is truly confident. It may be hard to identify more than a few confident individuals—maybe even only one. That is a good thing—proof that confident people are unique and make positive, lasting impressions. They aren't a dime a dozen—and, as a result, they not only command your attention, they tend to be more successful in all aspects of life from wealth to well-being.

Now with that confident person in mind, ask yourself this question:

What makes that person *look* confident?

When doing presentations and workshops, I hear a relatively consistent list of answers from audience members. They report that confident people:

- stand tall
- dress sharply and are well-groomed
- look comfortable
- present a strong handshake
- maintain good eye contact
- listen well and are not distracted
- smile genuinely

When I ask what confident people *do*, these are the answers I most often hear.

Confident people:

- listen better
- are listened to better
- are diplomatic but decisive
- don't get upset
- don't get emotional
- don't judge
- apologize appropriately
- are eager to learn
- they conscientiously solicit and consider feedback

Take a moment to consider if these characteristics map back to the confident person you are analyzing. Do these attributes match?

Some workshop participants will say a confident person appears to "feel comfortable in his or her own skin." This observation highlights that confident people are sure about who they are and what they want to portray. They say and behave in ways that are commensurate to their own definition of self—which in turn conveys a calm control and comfort in their outward persona.

> *"The greatest gifts you can give yourself and others are not presents but 'presence'."*
>
> Alyssa Dver

Now the big question: *How do you compare with your confident role model and the attributes noted above?*

Answering that question honestly will allow you to begin uncovering your own confidence strengths and weaknesses. And if you are truly genuine with yourself, you should be confessing a bit because you know that you could—or perhaps should - be more confident.

Congratulations! This isn't as grave as Alcoholics Anonymous but like most formal self-improvement programs, the first step to make real, lasting improvements is to honestly recognize your own shortcomings—in this case, acknowledging you could benefit from improving your confidence at least some.

However, even if you are reading this and saying, "Nope, I'm good. I already got this, thank you," please consider how knowing more about confidence can help your kids, nieces and nephews, or someone you manage or mentor.

Therefore, let's unmask how the more common "not confident" people act and the implications of their behavior on them and everyone else. Regardless of how or why they are not confident, our concern is what they do and how we can deal with it better—and avoid doing those things ourselves.

# Confidence Imposters

It would then seem likely that doing the same exercise we just did to examine a confident person would yield the opposite answers on some we know that is NOT confident. In fact, all the answers are the opposite with a few major differences:

1. "Not confident" people are the norm.

2. "Not confident" people try to mimic confident people and it actually makes them appear even less confident. For example, they may have a fake smile or make intermittent eye contact.

3. People who are not confident, especially those who attempt to fake confidence, are visibly uncomfortable in the presence of someone who is confident. Confident people don't change based on who they interact with!

I use "not confident" because everyone is insecure in at least some areas of life and I don't believe that is negative. If you acknowledge personal weaknesses, this is an ultimately a sign of confidence. What I do consider negative is denying or being ignorant of your values, your behaviors and/or your impact on others. Thus, the first step to becoming more confident is identifying and being more vigilant of insecurities that impact your own and other people's performances.

To start, let's peel apart some personality traits that often are construed as confidence but are actually fake impressions of real confidence—I call them *confidence imposters*. These personality types are not only often mistaken for confidence; they actually reflect a lack of confidence.

I bet you know a bunch of people who are like this:

- **Cocky** – someone who brags about his or her abilities/possessions/relationships/activities

- **One Upper** – someone who often needs to say or prove he or she is better than others in specific ways. Typically, this one-upmanship is verbal and can come in the form of something the individual claims they did, someone important they know or something they say they have

- **Indifferent** – someone who is seemingly uninterested either on purpose or due to an inability to focus

- **Perpetually pissed** – someone who appears angry all the time and puts up a defensive face or attitude to ensure other people keep a distance

- **Pedantically nice** – someone who offers to seemingly always help or just listen without limits or needing reciprocity, but has an ulterior motive other than being charitable. Life coaches call this being disingenuous.

> *"I'm disappointed when a liar's pants*
> *don't actually catch on fire."*
>
> Sylvester the Cat

It is very likely that you know people who fall into one or more of those categories. Perhaps in the past you perceived those personalities as confident. However, if you review the previous list of confident characteristics against the imposter's behavior, you will see the truth. Confidence is not about being aloof or sweet. It's not about being able to brag comfortably or putting yourself before other people.

People who are not confident often try to raise their own confidence by negating other people. An example of this is someone who feels personally deprived when someone else reports a big promotion or new car. The insecure listener will congratulate the other person half-heartedly, and inevitably display his or her thoughts of "Why him and why not me?" Insecure people are prone to gossiping and will talk behind a winner's back, saying, "She really doesn't deserve it" or "She must have done something unacceptable to get it." These sentiments imply that the successful person cheated, slept with the boss, bribed someone or did some other unprofessional thing in order to achieve success. Rather than be a supportive colleague and learn from the winner's success, "not confident" people often internalize the other person's win as something that is wrong with the world, not with their own behavior.

> *"Always remember that you are absolutely unique.*
> *Just like everyone else."*
>
> Margaret Mead

There are even the personality types that solicit too much feedback to confirm to themselves that they are socially accepted. It can be annoying to give a person like this endless kudos. It is so obviously clear that the solicitor is insecure and needy that you may even feel sorry for that empty individual.

If we could simply ignore or avoid these imposters, we wouldn't have to respond to them and thereafter regret how we did. While it is rarely a conscious attitude, imposters love to raise their own confidence by reducing someone else's. Never let an imposter deflate your confidence. Now that you have the imposter profiles, keep a look out and when encountering such people, just breathe. Remember, the toxic comments, indifference and obsequious, yet scheming attitude, are the result of the other individual's confidence suffocating.

> *"Insecurity will always rent the space it occupies,*
> *but confidence will own the building,*
> *and any other room it steps in."*
>
> Azgraybebly Josland

# Bonehead Behaviors

A half-hearted congratulation is a good example of a *bonehead behavior*. I define a bonehead behavior as an action that unintentionally shows insecurity. We have all had to suffer other people's bonehead behaviors, and it's most likely we've also done them ourselves.

Examples of bonehead behaviors:

- Gossiping

- Mean/condescending/demanding bosses

- Interrupting a meeting or conversation to answer our electronic devices (except for a legitimate emergency)

- CC'ing 'all' or many others on a memo that only one person really needs to receive

- Acting 'macho' (even if you are a woman) or in accordance to a personal style that is not your own to fit in a team/group/level

- Seeming to be indifferent to something that is obviously important to other people

There are many more bonehead behaviors, but here are two common ones that are worthy of more than a bullet.

The first is what I call, "**Pucker Face**." The opposite is a *poker face* which means that someone doesn't transmit his or her thoughts or emotions in any form of facial or body language. A poker-faced person literally hides behind a non-expressive façade. A *pucker face*, on the flip side, is when someone looks pissed pretty much all the time and deliberately transmits to the world that she or he is not happy. They have sunken cheeks and a general scowl. They are clearly communicating even without words, "Go ahead, make my day...I dare you." It's a warning much like a snarl or stare down.   It is an unfortunately common sight you may see walking into a meeting or dealing with someone one on one. That pucker-faced person is communicating silently, "Don't mess with me because I am not confident."

While we can't blindly guess why these people act like this, it is usually easy to soften them by simply being nice: smile, say hello and make small talk. It turns out that their silent bark is usually worse than their verbal bite. When you kick back with kindness not fear or anger, these people tend to back down, and may surprise you with friendliness and often loyalty. However, just like with a dog (as much as I am a dog lover), you have to always be vigilant.  There is a deeper reason why these people are perpetually pissed and they may bite at any moment—they may say harsh words to you or behind your back. These responses are not always with intention, but because of learned reaction. Therefore, to deal with them in the here and now, and to avoid becoming a sour puss yourself, just smother them with confidence and you just may be pleased to see how they heel.

A second, all too common, bonehead behavior is *smartest person in the room* syndrome. Smart people are prone to this—including, smart, *successful* people. In a discussion between two or more people, one person often feels the need to declare him or herself the smartest. He or she does this by correcting the other person ("No, that is not correct"), or by deliberately talking at a level that is pompous (e.g. "I am sure that you are familiar with Yeats' translation of Sophocles"). To deal with this type of behavior, acknowledge the smarty-pants comment politely and confidently by saying something along the lines of, "Thank you, Joseph. I did not know that." Then continue in your conversation. That small acknowledgment of Joseph's "contribution" and your confident statement will often be enough to prevent him from making further deliberately alienating comments. Then, if he makes the same bonehead comment again, it will be with your consent and not at your emotional expense.

A confident person does not feel a need to impress others, and doesn't degrade other people in a discussion. Of course there are times when it may be necessary to use jargon or somewhat arcane words for the sake of descriptive accuracy. However, if communication fails at the cost of trying to make someone feel incompetent, what is the speaker or writer really impressing? Remember that big words do not equal big confidence.

So next time someone decides to be the smartest person in the room, or you walk into a meeting and are presented with a pucker face, realize it's those people's insecurity on display. Take it as their 'tell' and that your competitive strategy is to stay on a confident course and not fall victim to their bonehead traps. Those individuals actually want to bring you to their lower level of confidence. Often unconsciously, they try to push you down so they can get the upper hand. Don't fall for it. Stand up, be mindful and know that you can maintain confidence despite these off-putting, imposter behaviors.

> *"Be who you are and say what you feel, because those who mind don't matter and those who matter don't mind."*
>
> Dr. Seuss

# Confidence Cousins

There are many psychological and neurological terms that are closely related to confidence. We'll kick the tires of some here knowing that the subject of confidence drives an infinite number of related topics. It is perhaps why there is so little yet known and taught about confidence specifically, let alone how to condition and control it.

The first most related cousin to discuss is *self-esteem*. Dictionary.com defines self-esteem as *"a realistic respect for or favorable impression of oneself."*[12] Self-esteem is a hotly debated topic studied by tons of surveys, research and psycho-social professionals. In the past decade, there has been a movement to promote the importance of building self-esteem, especially in children and teens. From Dove commercials[13] to in-school assemblies, our society actively promotes feeling good about yourself just because "you're worth it."[14]

Now, however, many pundits argue that self-esteem creates false pretenses about one's capabilities, and subsequently an inability to survive without the critical life skills of being resourceful and resilient. Giving children compliments about the beautiful fish they just caught turns out to be less helpful then constructively complimenting how they actually caught the fish. Recognizing 'how' they did something rather that 'what they did' allows them to apply the lessons to other circumstances. This makes them better equipped to perform other tasks optimally—as well as cope and recover from failures.

> *"Thus, high self-esteem may refer to an accurate, justified, balanced appreciation of one's worth as a person and one's successes and competencies, but it can also refer to an inflated, arrogant, grandiose, unwarranted sense of conceited superiority over others. By the same token, low self-esteem can be either an accurate, well-founded understanding of one's shortcomings as a person or a distorted, even pathological sense of insecurity and inferiority."*
>
> *Excerpted from:* "Does High Self-esteem Cause Better Performance, Interpersonal Success, Happiness, or Healthier Lifestyles?" *Baumeister, R.F., Campbell, J.D., Krueger, J.I. and Vohs, J.D.* [15]

Even more recently, many experts now proclaim that *self-compassion* is the more important trait. Knowing how to "cut yourself some slack" is a critical life skill. If you are self-compassionate, you allow yourself to fail and thereafter, you are more likely to get back on the horse after being kicked off. A self-compassionate individual is humble enough to know when they aren't a competitive rider and they may go and try another sport. Someone with "just" self-esteem will either keep trying in vain or simply blame external factors for their own inability. They are unable to deal productively with the feelings of failure, and may walk away from trying anything else from fear of future failure.

*Self-efficacy* is another trait related to confidence. It is a belief that you can do or achieve something—a specific task or goal. It is a key component of confidence yet is only a subset since confidence also requires an alignment to your values. Just because you "can" do something, doesn't mean you want to or should. I know I can jump off a bridge but that doesn't mean I will, should or want to.

*Courage* is associated with confidence since it is a reaction or response to the anticipated likelihood of success when doing a specific thing. Having the courage to say or do something takes into consideration the historical outcomes and perceived necessary knowledge, plus other factors specific to the current situation. In some ways, having courage implies you are willing to blindly jump in and just do. Perhaps absolute courage is to take on a physical or moral challenge even without careful preparation or understanding. Courage assumes you may receive pain or some negative result, but you do the act despite it, if not in ignorance. Confidence, on the other hand, is more controlled and thoughtful. Confidence is a surety of what is right and no matter what happens, it is conviction about what is the best course of action.

> *"Your time is limited, so don't waste it living someone else's life. Don't be trapped by dogma—which is living with the results of other people's thinking. Don't let the noise of others' opinions drown out your own inner voice. And most importantly, have the courage to follow your heart and intuition."*
>
> Steve Jobs

You can have confidence and not the courage to do something—especially if there is a risk that it may compromise your values. You can actually have courage and not real confidence (like, say, the Cowardly Lion from *The Wizard of Oz*[16]). Courage tends to be temporal or situational. Confidence is ideally more consistent. Core confidence helps ensure that consistency and (follow me on this as its confusing): if your courage is being tested, core confidence will help you stay aligned with your values and beliefs.

Confidence is really about holding true to yourself, rather than deviating into something that will risk your safety, morals and/or integrity.

The last confidence cousin is *resilience*. While core confidence enables resilience, resilience on its own isn't the same thing. A clear example is people who easily "let things roll off their back." Resilient individuals seemingly don't let other people's issues or angst impact their own lives. At times, resilience may be viewed as being unemotionally attached, but confident people use their values conscientiously to choose what to attach to and what to let be.

Confident resilience is also about having the ability to recover from a setback. People in occupational transition experience a grief-like cycle of emotions. People who experience this loss but choose to move on are those who will more easily find work—especially desirable work. Individuals who are overlooked for a promotion can choose to linger in self-pity or opt to identify what they can do when future opportunities come along. It's not about finding silver linings but more importantly, about getting golden growing lessons.

Carol Dweck's pinnacle work on growth mindsets[17] clearly supports the important skill of resilience. On her *Mindset* website, she notes, "Beyond how traumatic a setback can be in the fixed mindset, this mindset gives you no good recipe for overcoming it. If failure means you lack competence or potential—that you are a failure—where do you go from there?" Dweck pulls examples from sports as well as business, teaching, parenting and all other type of relationships to illustrate the power of learning from our mistakes to become high-performance individuals. Her work is now commonplace in educational and professional training to help people expand their minds and attitudes.

One common way to have resilience is to believe in a higher power. Religion or any sense of fate provides some kind of an explanation so that we can gain some confidence and closure to move forward. If you consider the result of faith being resilience and less about the method to get there, the technique is no less honorable than manning up and just picking yourself up by your bootstraps. Permit yourself to use whatever confidence empowering method works to get you "past the past."

> *"Resilient people consider mistakes as experiences for learning and growth."*
>
> *Excerpted from: "The Power to Change Your Life: Ten Keys to Resilient Living." Brooks, R.* [18]

Being resilient is certainly a desired human trait. We want the ability to bounce back from setbacks and to avoid future problems. We want to be bulletproof like Superman and not let anything stick to us, even under fire, like Teflon-coated pans. Yet, the only way to really do this in our everyday lives is to build and maintain strong core confidence. In so doing, we won't avoid hardships or challenges, but we can more easily leap over seemingly tall obstacles and allow undesirable residue to more easily slip off our backs.

> *"A confident person appreciates the view,*
> *even on a detour."*
>
> Anonymous

Confidence gives us the wisdom to know that sometimes humans make mistakes or are just unlucky. Confidence also gives us the humility to laugh and learn from mistakes so we can get better with age—not so much as a fine wine that mellows, but more like a good cheese that gets stronger over time. Cheese, unlike wine, knows how to productively use the surrounding air to increase the cheese's distinction without spoiling the ripe character. With strong core confidence, you too can act like a big cheese full of interesting character. Whether interacting with confidence imposters, or simply taking the time to be introspective, start proactively using all of life's opportunities to grow and cultivate confidence.

Now with a hopeful hunger for building confidence, let's start by understanding some baseline confidence facts.

# Confidence Consensus

*"As...as we humbly accept our place as one amongst our fellow human beings, mindfully acknowledging that we all have self-doubt, we all suffer, we all fail from time to time, but none of that means we can't live a life of meaning, purpose, and compassion for ourselves and others."*

Excerpted from an article: "Is Self Compassion More Important Than Self Esteem?" Haynes, S. [19]
By Steven C. Hayes, Ph.D.

In 2013, we started ACI by surveying 192 individuals online. The respondents ranged in age from 20-75 with variances in people who were parents, who worked, who lived in different places and had zero to many siblings. The objective was to get a sense of how people felt about their confidence and what they subjectively felt contributed to it. We wanted to provide some confidence baseline data across the group but we also hoped to see if the responses varied between genders, ages or other demographic variables.

The results were reassuring and perhaps obvious:

- When asked to rate their own confidence, men rated their own higher than women did.
- Confidence increases as we age—it is strongest after 45 and maintains that strength thereafter.
- Strong relationships and personal support systems are critical to being confident and maintaining confidence.

- Health and well-being contribute highly to one's confidence.
- Many millennials (18-24) hang on to some teenage angst with regards to how they look and who they impress.
- Women attempt balance across all aspects of their career and personal lives, but overwhelmingly focus on their own physical attributes for a confidence boost.
- Men indicate street smarts, sexual relations and their families' appearance and behavior as top factors in their confidence.

See the following infographics for more survey details:

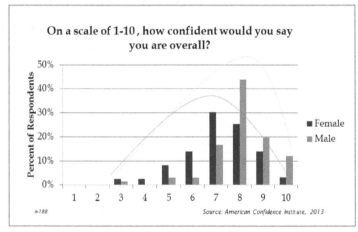

1 = low confidence 10 = high confidence

Key takeaway:

✓ Most women rate their confidence around a 7 (majority between 6-9) while men think more "highly" of their confidence at an 8 (majority between 7-10).

Kickass Confidence: Confidence Consensus

How we rate our own confidence

1= lowest confidence, 10 = highest

Age 18
6
Age 25
5-7
Age 35
7
Age 45
8
Age 55+
8

Parents tend to rate their confidence higher than adults without children.

There was no difference in confidence rating among people who worked full-time, part-time or were full-time parents.

Key takeaway:

✓ Our confidence changes over time, peaking at about age 45.

## Age and Confidence

What gives us confidence changes as we age

What contributes most to confidence:

**Age 18-24**
- clothing
- friendships
- education/academic achievement/book smarts

**Age 25-34**
- financial control

**Age 35-44**
- overall career achievement

**Age 44+**
- partner/spouse relationships
- physical health

Key takeaway:

✓ What feeds our confidence changes over time.

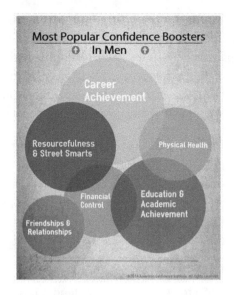

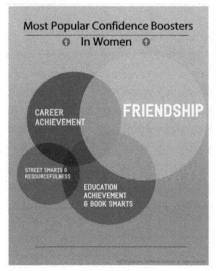

Key takeaway:

✓   Men have more factors that feed their confidence and they
    are different than what feeds women's confidence.

Most people aren't surprised by these results but are reassured to know their own confidence is 'normal'. It also helps orient us to know what confidence factors are important. Subsequently, we know that the things that feed our confidence actually change over time. Our confidence isn't a fixed container maintaining the same volume or shape.

Confidence is largely a reflection of a society and its particular priorities and propaganda—what we are told through advertising, our parents, teachers and friends. The ultimate accomplishment is being able to identify what and why something is important to you—even if the reason is "just because."

Conclusively, everyone has confidence issues in one or more areas of life. As we age, we tend to give up fighting with ourselves about our deficiencies, and tend to come to acknowledge our gifts. With years of gained certainty, we know that like that smelly cheese, we too are fine.

Meanwhile, if we are lucky, we figure out sooner rather than too late what is really important to us. Those that are luckier still, may have the courage to uphold those values. This is what makes us more comfortable in our own skin—even (or as a result of) being wrinkled and transparent. Perhaps the truest sign of growing up is when you are finally unapologetic about who you are and what rocks and roots you.

> "I know myself now, and I feel within me a peace above all earthly dignities, a still and quiet conscience."
>
> William Shakespeare [20]

# Confident Mindfulness

Mindfulness is in. It's a hot topic in books, magazines, blogs, corporate wellness programs and other channels. Mindfulness means being aware of the world around us. It is the presence of mind to know our current place in the world. According to some definitions, mindfulness also includes the appreciation of what we have done in the past and will do in the future. Ways to be more mindful include meditation, yoga, massage and all other forms of relaxation such that your mind is free to think and observe. Whether you are a millennial or soon to retire, most of us are often overwhelmed and seek calm and control through a variety of methods. Many of these could be qualified as ways to become more mindful.

For decades, executive and life coaches have known that self-awareness is a key to improving one's self-control, leadership and overall impact. Techniques such as 360 evaluations, a plethora of personality assessments and numerous coaching modalities all have the same thread of helping a client become more self-aware.

Sports coaches also recognize self-awareness as a key to helping athletes manage their emotions so that they can proactively identify and control internal or external distractions. Using mindfulness techniques to obtain peak performance is now a common element of elite athletic training.

Long before coaches realized the benefits of being centered, Eastern medicine followed the premise that managing—or at least appreciating—your own mind was the most powerful tool of all. Thousands of books have been written extoling the benefits of various forms of mindfulness and the direct correlation to one's well-being and performance.

Mindfulness does also bolster confidence. Specifically, two very common techniques are used regularly by high performance individuals. One is the concept of 'structures' and the second is achieving "small wins." Let's discuss both briefly as they apply to building your own confidence.

ACI's experienced Chief Coaching Officer, Lynnette Rumble defines a structure as "an object, phrase, word, action or process which immediately reminds you of a certain mindset, value, belief or other core sense. This concrete item is a reminder of your core value or beliefs and provides a confident 'power surge' or a powerful ritual that then connects your beliefs with your behavior."

Supporting this, research from Harvard professors Michael Norton and Francesca Gino shows that rituals have the power to make you more confident. Francesca states:

> "What we studied in this project was whether these rituals are really of beneficial effect in terms of bringing you confidence and potentially impacting your performance positively. That is actually what we found. What is interesting about the studies is that we also have physiological measures. What we find is that if you engage in a ritual prior to a potentially high-anxiety task, like singing in public or solving difficult math problems, you end up being calmer by the time you approach the task and more confident in what you're about to do. As a result of that, you actually perform better."[20]

In all modalities of life coaching, structures are used to create a concrete process for a client to stay on task. A structure maybe something conventional such as a checklist or app, or it can be more personal like a photo or keepsake.

Lucky charms are actually structures. Robert Biswas-Diener, author of *The Courage Quotient: How Science Can Make You Braver*, notes:

> *"The researchers found that by activating good-luck beliefs, these objects were consistently able to boost people's self-confidence and that this uptick in self-assurance, in turn, affected a wide range of performance. Lucky thinking, it turned out in this study, positively affected people's ability to solve puzzles and to remember the pictures depicted on 36 different cards, and it improved their putting performance in golf! In fact, people with a lucky charm performed significantly better than did the people who had none. That's right, having a lucky charm will make you a better golfer, should you care about such things, and improve your cognitive performance on tasks such as memory games."* [22]

Structures help connect individuals to a particular thought process/state of mind/positive feeling that can provide powerful, ritual-based behavior. For example, the client looks at a photo of himself/herself accepting an award of excellence during times when he/she feels a need to remember the strength of one's own knowledge base. Michael Phelps, Dustin Pedroias and dozens of other athletes have notorious, consistent and very visible preparation habits that are in fact, structures.

A second mindfulness approach that helps build confidence is to deliberately plan and achieve "small wins." Many Olympic athletes train in this way to specifically build confidence. Rather than focusing on the gold medal, they set smaller achievable goals and build from there. Daniel Chambliss, PhD and author of a number of books including, *Champions: The Making of Olympic Swimmers* [23], tracked the techniques used by the USA National Swim Team over the course of a year to prepare its athletes to compete in the Olympic Games. One of the common threads in this training was to focus on a series of small wins in training rather than on the larger goal of winning a medal.

As Chambliss summarized it, the swimmers "found their challenges in small things: working on a better start this week, polishing up their backstroke technique next week, planning how to pace their swim." As a result, they received the satisfaction of "very definable, minor achievements," which in turn, gave them the confidence to attempt additional small wins each and every day.

Breaking down larger goals is an important piece of any project management so that you aren't overwhelmed by trying to tackle everything at once. Taking on small wins helps make it more manageable and you compound more and more confidence as you go!

Another interesting mindful perspective is that confidence isn't something that is a result, but rather it is something you do to achieve a result. Elliott Newell, PhD in sport psychology contends that "confidence is not an emotion; we can't feel it. It is a belief; this makes it a thought."

Some of the confidence tips Newell encourages high performance athletes to consider include:

1. Stop trying to feel confident and start thinking 'confident.'

2. Devise strategies that make confidence (on competition day) an expectation rather than a hope.

3. Confidence is multi-dimensional. High confidence in one area does not mean you have high confidence in all areas. Understand and develop the many different types of confidence and your overall confidence will take care of itself.

4. Understand where your confidence comes from. Once your sources of confidence are understood, you can take more ownership of your overall confidence. *e.g. "My confidence is high when I am well prepared."*

5. Build confidence from the bottom up rather than the top down. Do this by targeting various sources of confidence rather than approaching it from the perspective of building confidence overall.

> *"It is possible that, like a muscle exercised over time, experiencing positive emotions in daily life (hedonic well-being) can produce important long-term benefits (eudemonic well-being) (cf., Fredrickson, 2000). We have found that cultivating positive emotions (exercising the muscle) Is important for promoting resilience (a personal strength)."*
>
> Excerpted from: "Regulation of Positive Emotions: Emotion Regulation Strategies That Promote Resilience."

Taking into account these mindfulness theories, let's dig deeper into cutting edge neuroscience and the connection between the Eastern and Western approaches to building confidence as they meet in the emerging field of neuroplasticity.

# The Science of Confidence

With ACI's collected evidence, we know that confidence can be a learned and deliberate thoughts and attitudes. Therefore, we propose that anyone can conscientiously increase confidence. We further propose that conditioned over time, you can induce functional changes to the brain so that it operates in a default, resilient state of confidence.

*If you are interested how this actually works in more scientific detail, please read on! If you prefer to just take my word that it does work, feel free to skip to the next chapters that explain what to do to strengthen your own core confidence.*

We've discussed how you can act as the "super admin" of your own brain and direct it to think and respond. You can even bargain with your own brain. We see this ability developed and used successfully by well-trained athletes and other high performance professionals—as well as by my own son, Zak. These individuals all induced neuroplasticity so they could ultimately have more control of their thoughts and movements. They learned how to be more self-aware and in total control of the connections between their inevitable emotions and desired motions.

However, there is the lingering question whether you can actually change the way your brain works so it automatically thinks confidently. Like your involuntary breath and heartbeat, can you program your mind to be confident without having to deliberately self-talk or even consciously think? Can you increase your confidence no matter your experiences, intelligence and abilities?

The growing body of research and data about confidence includes Shipman and Kay's, *The Confidence Code*, and other books, plus dozens of neuroscience and psychological studies and articles. You can find many of these resources on the ACI website and in this book's bibliography. Executive/business and life coaches also work towards the common underlying goal of helping clients gain sustainable confidence through various methodologies. Motivational speakers and writers circle in and around confidence, often mixing in colors of the confidence cousins discussed previously.

The current cross-discipline thought leadership can be summarized as follows:

- Confidence isn't genetic.
- Confidence is a thought or state of thought, not a feeling or emotion.
- There are specific centers in the brain that are responsible for processing and creating confidence.
- It seems possible to strengthen those centers just like memory and concentration.

If you are familiar with the products and approach of Lumosity[3], you know it uses neuroplasticity to condition memory. To build stronger brain pathways, the theory and much clinical proof indicates that you can strengthen cognitive functions in the same conceptual way you condition muscles: through awareness and repetitive practice (akin to building muscle memory). While the brain does not visibly bulk up like muscles do, functional magnetic resonance images (MRIs that capture activity, not just form or matter) provide evidence that you can physically change the structures in the brain and make the neural pathways "stronger."

Beyond our previous definition of 'human' confidence, it is helpful to understand how neuroscientists and other technical professionals, such as statisticians and economists, break down confidence into discrete behaviors and actions. This helps explain the components of confidence and the discrete steps that enable our brains to process information that in turn, dictates how we think and act. Consider the brain to be just like a computer. Computers take in data and directions and then process that information to deliver an answer or to trigger another process. Our brains use information, including historical and forecasted data, to direct our bodies to deliver a result such as "move," "feel" or follow a thought.

To create a confident thought, our brains first analyze the options available given a specific decision, action or task. Then, your brain does a sub-second collection of options regarding what you *could* do.

The brain's second step is to evaluate the potential outcomes or consequences for each option—though only sometimes do you get the luxury of time to consciously consider all the potential outcomes. More often, it is a quick, seemingly subconscious, decision using data from learned experiences and/or what we consider to be common sense.

Next, the brain chooses the perceived best possible option in that moment of time. Again, this happens so quickly that most often, it doesn't even seem like a decision but rather just a rational, logical thought. Remember that the brain is just like a computer as it runs through all the known options and outcomes to determine the best-seeming scenario. And like a computer, our brain can only use the information it has. However, unlike a computer, we can recognize when desired information is lacking. This is what "chips away" at our confidence—the uncertainty of whether the selected action will likely result in the predicted or hopeful result.

Lastly, the brain then correlates one's own ability (self-efficacy) to actually carry out the option selected by weighing the likelihood of success.

In this multi-step process, our brains help us decide—often in a split second—whether we should, can or will do something based on the information we have, the attention we apply and the experiences we learned from.

> *"Choice certainty—the degree to which a decision-maker believes a choice is likely to be correct—affects a variety of cognitive functions: how we plan subsequent actions, how we react and learn from mistakes, and how we justify our choices to others."*
>
> Excerpted from: "Representation of Confidence Associated with a Decision by Neurons in the Parietal Cortex." Kiani, R. and Shadlen, M.[25]

Some experts also extend the confidence process to consider the post-action response from a decision made. For example, if you failed at something, this will certainly impact the confidence of that decision in hindsight and of course, it could impact future, related decisions. A bad investment in the stock market may make you more wary of investing in the future. However, as you probably know from your own or other people's investing, some people just don't let a past failure factor into their future confidence—for better or worse.

Science is also helping us understand how our brains and bodies are connected. One way is through quantitatively measuring stress to obtain a productive level of it. Contrary to what may seem logical, some stress is actually needed for a person to be confident and reach peak performance. Athletes have long known that there is a crucial amount of stress needed to unlock adrenaline, get blood flowing and get muscles ready. Consider it the desired state of fight versus fright. With this heightened sense of preparedness, athletes learn how to build and manage appropriate stress *on demand*.

Using tried and true biofeedback tools can therefore measure stress by monitoring pulse, sweat, and other vital markers.

It is also relatively common that executive functions can be measured and strengthened to help individuals focus and be more thoughtful. Technology today can measure brain waves as they change from front of the brain/executive function (prefrontal cortex) to the back of the brain (cerebrum and brainstem) that manage autonomic functions such as breathing and heartbeat. Brain waves identify when someone is in a more mindful state versus a more involuntary and potentially stressful state.

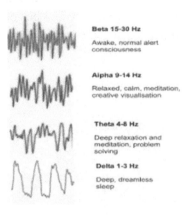

Brain wave illustration courtesy of http://geraldguild.com/blog

Well-trained yogis, monks and other meditation practitioners are known for their ability to control their brain waves and subsequently their body functions. With proper mindfulness training, some individuals can regulate their pulse, temperature and other vital signs. The techniques to do this often involve visualization and other structures that have been practiced, or perhaps more accurately "programmed", into the memory muscle in the person's mind. Like swinging a golf club until it is rote or practicing anything for at least 10,000 hours as Malcolm Gladwell[25] professes, mastery comes from automating the neural connections between mind and body.

Other Eastern mindfulness methods can have the same effect – from acupuncture to tai chi and yoga. The same concepts apply here: enable a quiet, controlled brain that in turn gives better control to the body and all its thoughts and actions.

Neuroscientists are also discovering where and how our brains process complex cognitive functions such as memory and confidence. In this quest, they are only beginning to understand how to build or rebuild those functions using both technology and/or technique. The promise is that with more research, we will be able to use our own brains to heal, or at least improve, our health and well-being – including our core confidence.

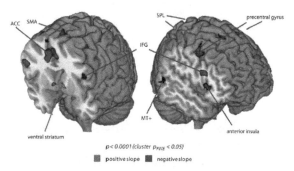

*An example of how functional magnetic imaging helps identify areas of the brain that contribute to confidence.*

*Excerpted from: "The relationship between perceptual decision variables and confidence in the human brain." Hebart, M., Schriever, Y., Donner, T. and Haynes, J-D.*[26]

Meanwhile, scientists and doctors have made huge progress in helping the brain function 'better' despite damage or disability.

For example, some individuals who suffer from neurological damage or dysfunction can benefit from Deep Brain Stimulation (DBS). DBS is essentially a pacemaker for your brain. Surgically implanted and expertly calibrated, DBS generates electrical impulses in specific regions in the brain that then change the body's physical movements. As described in the Foreword of the book, dystonia is a description for one condition caused by neurological disconnects. DBS has been used to treat some more debilitating cases of dystonia by successfully enabling muscular control. DBS is also being investigated as a possible treatment for movement disorders including Parkinson's, Multiple Sclerosis, Obsessive Compulsive Disorder (OCD), and Tourette's.

Other forms of less invasive brain stimulation are also starting to emerge as potential treatments including Magnetic Resonance Therapy (MRT) and Transcranial Magnetic Stimulation (TMS) or Transcranial Direct Magnetic Stimulation (TDMS). These techniques are starting to show promising results for patients with depression, autism and chronic pain.

Medications are also commonly used to either enhance or suppress brain activity. For example, Parkinson's patients use a variety of drugs that essentially help the brain better control movements of the body, while ADHD patients use different medication to enable cerebral focus and control.

It turns out that alcohol is sometimes a doctor-recommended 'medication' used to help some patients by desensitizing a brain that is overactive, or clearly out of the person's control. Being tipsy doesn't enable control but the right amount of alcohol can actually help relax the brain and it can subsequently reduce neurological conflicts happening between mind and body. However, alcohol is considered "liquid courage" not because it gives us more cognitive control, but because it can also remove undesirable interpersonal inhibitions!

Any one of these 'prescriptions' may help someone at least temporarily. However, like most things, there are pros and cons, including cost, convenience, as well as short and long term side effects. Therefore, the quest to find an all-encompassing solution prevails.

*Neuroplasticity appears to be a powerful puzzle piece.*

It is likely that someday soon, patients with neurological movement disorders will ultimately gain more control of their brains and subsequently their muscles, without complete dependency on drugs or invasive devices. Even other conditions, from obesity to Post Traumatic Stress Disorder (PSTD), depression and Attention Deficit Hyperactivity Disorder (ADHD), could be potentially helped by the patient reprogramming his/her own brain and building stronger or alternative neuropathways. Dozens of case studies are available including video footage of before and after results using non-invasive, therapeutic techniques. The therapies focus on teaching and reinforcing new ways to process movement and memory—basically building or rebuilding the connections between brain and body that have been compromised because of genetics, medications, stress, chemicals, or other toxic factors.

Neuroplasticity-based training techniques are already being employed by peak performing individuals such as top military personnel, as well as professional and Olympic athletes. Using repetitive mindful conditioning, the athletes/soldiers become more self-aware and able to maintain focus. These high performance individuals have the 'muscle memory' to quickly identify and deal with distraction by consciously moving their thoughts from back of their brains to the front where they have executive control and clarity. Through this mindful process, the individuals learn when and how to reach peak stress/arousal and to know when and how to return to it if they are side tracked. In this way, without an electrical or magnetic shock of the brain, they efficiently build the neural pathways required for the athlete or soldier to obtain and sustain concentration, control and subsequently, confidence.

If you read the book or saw the movie *Divergent*, you may recall the climatic training required by the Divergent sector recruits. After other types of courage-building and confidence-stabilizing lessons, the rookies are put into a special simulation room and injected with an unknown drug. The recruits find themselves in a seemingly realistic version of their worst nightmare. The training is meant to create the most stressful situation possible for that specific individual. The trainers meanwhile measure how long it takes for the recruit to find a solution and successfully break free of the virtual situation. The process is done over again until the recruit eventually learns from his or her mistakes and figures out how to overcome their fears and associated stress. Only then can they take control quickly and break out of the nightmare. Though *Divergent* is a work of fiction, it adequately captures the spirit of the stressful state and techniques to overcome them. Lucky for us, inducing neuroplasticity doesn't have to require pain or anxiety.

And yes, I have witnessed it with my own eyes, with my own son. Beyond what I saw on the tennis court for years, Zak's dystonia was "cured" in four short non-invasive therapeutic sessions. With gentle and intentional movements with his upper body, the therapy reintroduced his brain to doing things the way *he* wanted to do them, not the way his *brain* thought was correct. He was changing the way his brain had previously and somehow incorrectly learned to do certain movements.

We'll never really know what caused his brain to learn the 'wrong' patterns of movement. Maybe it was due to anxiety or physical stress. Perhaps it was like so many musicians and artists that develop dystonia such as writers' cramp that prevents them from performing the craft that they have intensely mastered. Dystonia all of a sudden causes them to have both a painful physical and mental lack of control that prevents these highly perceptive, gifted 'movement experts' from practicing or performing their art.

One theory is that the individuals have inadvertently trained their bodies in some incorrect form, and subsequently their brains are following the incorrect pattern. Another theory states that their brains have been neurologically damaged by stress that shocked the brain and derailed the normal neuropathways that control the correct movement of those muscles. For whatever cause, many of these individuals, including Zak, have been able to retrain their brains so their muscles and minds are in sync and follow the desired, "non-dysfunctional", directions. They are able to take control by essentially being the super admins of their own their bodies. They reprogrammed the neurological movement instructions coming from their brains to conduct the complex orchestra of their muscles.

Conclusively, if the brain also has specific centers and pathways that process confidence, it stands to reason that you can also strengthen those neural pathways to control desired outcomes. In ACI's coaching and workshop experiences, this has been true. Using simple coaching tools and techniques, we believe that you can consciously and quantitatively improve your core confidence.

Like the Olympic diver who does a quick self-check before mounting the platform, you, too, can learn to identify and rectify areas in your life that cause confidence deficits. You can increase confidence by identifying and dealing with deficits while also celebrating confidence credits! Over time, you'll even preempt confidence derailments from even happening and making "confidence" a default thought and state of being. Using ACI's Confidence Conditioning process, you can build a strong base of core confidence. Afterwards, you may even laugh at your own and other people's bonehead behaviors.

# Confidence Conditioning

We recognize that in today's "always busy" world, few people have the time or patience to read, sit in a long lecture or complete complex questionnaires. It's pretty unreasonable these days to ask anyone to do a lengthy personality or other personal assessment and then remember his/her own and everyone else's scores to apply them. It's also misleading to take a generalized characteristic such as "introvert" and ubiquitously apply it to how someone should live or work.

ACI's confidence conditioning process is indeed mindful of these issues and aims to give you not so much a series of to do's as much as a new perspective about your own and other people's confidence. With more effective filters and coping mechanisms, you can quickly build and sustain core confidence.

The approach presented here leverages the common coaching techniques of self-awareness, structures, small wins and accountability to induce neuroplasticity and achieve new, powerful confidence connections in the brain. Almost immediately, your default thoughts and resulting behaviors will be more assured and confident.

> *"There can be no happiness if the things we believe in are different than the things we do."*
>
> Blaise Pascal

Increasing confidence involves four steps and tools that will be explained in the next few chapters:

1) Assessing the current state of confidence by using 8 **Key Confidence Indicators (KCIs)**;

2) Using a structure called a **Personal Confidence Dashboard** to clearly see the areas of confidence that need attention;

3) Developing a **Personal Confidence Plan** with very specific, small win-sized actions that can quickly and visibly raise confidence.

4) Referring back to the Confidence Dashboard every few days until it is visually resident in the brain. You can do this on your own or with the help of a life coach to ensure accountability and/or make necessary adjustments due to changes in your life and needs.

> *"Confidence comes from stepping out of your comfort zone and working towards goals that come from your own values and needs, goals that aren't determined by society"*
>
> Caroline Miller
> as noted in *The Confidence Code* by Kay and Shipman[6]

The process should take you about 15 minutes initially and for the next few days thereafter, about 5 minutes. Soon, the process will become innate, and you will find yourself not only auto-calibrating your confidence regularly, but also you'll also catch yourself quickly if you veer off your desired confidence path.

When someone does a bonehead behavior, it may still poke at your confidence but instead of reacting with an equally regrettable behavior or thought, you'll stop yourself and regroup. When you are feeling overwhelmed or underappreciated, use the tools here to instantly gain inner and outer presence. Then remind yourself that confidence can be conditioned and like physical training, there are going to be good days and bad.

The ultimate sign that you are getting stronger is when you confidently know that you have the power to control your own thoughts and behaviors. It's that core conviction that definitively makes you know, "I got this."

# Key Confidence Indicators (KCIs)

Business performance is often measured and monitored by a set of Key Performance Indicators (KPIs). KPIs are tracked on dashboards to visually assess the health of the company or division. Using a combination of historical information together with forecasted measurements, the KPIs help identify healthy areas of the business or areas that need attention.

Likewise, **Key Confidence Indicators (KCIs)** help individuals assess and address areas of their own confidence well-being. Also like KPIs, they aren't necessarily prescriptive but rather they signal that a specific area needs attention. KCIs also help organize and prioritize an abundance of things we *could* do versus things we *should* do—and then manage those decisions over time through life's inevitable changing conditions.

Think of KCIs as containers or buckets of life priorities. If one bucket is less full than another, it may be because you consciously (or not) decided to keep it at that level or perhaps you haven't had time or energy to fill it higher. Not every bucket can be filled all the time (sorry to say—in reality, we really can't nor should have all priorities equally attended to). Often, one bucket must be focused on to the detriment of another, and, as is natural, priorities change over time. KCIs, therefore, are just a simple way to make more mindful meaningful decisions about how to spend your time, money and emotional energy.

Many people consider life balance as the foundation to living a happier, more confidence life. At ACI, we include more than just the footings of work and home but the Maslovian needs of love and social fulfillment in our lives.

At ACI, we identified 8 KCIs:

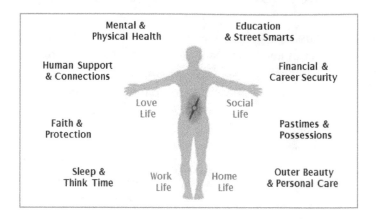

| | |
|---|---|
| Mental & Physical Health | Education & Street Smarts |
| Human Support & Connections | Financial & Career Security |
| Love Life | Social Life |
| Faith & Protection | Pastimes & Possessions |
| Sleep & Think Time | Outer Beauty & Personal Care |
| Work Life | Home Life |

Containing the complexities of life into 8 KCI buckets helps us more quickly, yet meaningfully, assess and address confidence areas.

Therefore, as the next step, we will briefly describe the definition and scope of each KCI so that you can fill in your own Personal Confidence Dashboard.

## KCI #1: Mental and Physical Health

It may be rather obvious that your mental or physical health impacts your confidence. When you aren't in great mental or physical shape, your confidence and overall well-being are compromised. While there may certainly be circumstances beyond our control, in many cases our well-being is a reflection of how well we take care of ourselves. This includes exercise, eating well and communicating well with other people who can appropriately help us work though physical and mental problems and concerns (e.g. doctors, social workers, friends, consultants, etc.). Few of us actually enjoy going to a doctor—especially if we suspect a problem. However, it can be quite empowering to finally make that appointment to see someone for help—even if you might receive a scary or burdensome diagnosis. Taking control of your health and doing something about the issue is courageous—and, subsequently builds confidence.

In fact, at some point in our lives, we have all been told by someone else to "go see a doctor." Responding to this advice, we may have been defensive or in denial of the problem. Why? Because admitting we need to get medical help opens up a Pandora's Box filled with human fears including acknowledging that we may be sick, or that the medical consultation may be inconvenient or potentially uncomfortable. Worse yet, we may fear hearing a bad prognosis or be embarrassed because the problem could have been avoided.

Usually, not knowing what is the problem is actually more stressful than knowing. Only after you know what is wrong, then you can try to correct the problem. You can pretend not to care, but your subconscious knows that you should take some action. Once you make that appointment, you hopefully feel somewhat relieved since you've taken control. With a clear diagnosis and treatment, your health and confidence is strengthened. Of course, if you receive a serious prognosis, that will challenge your confidence as well as your overall life. However, until you take that action to find out what the issue is, the illness and denial both wear down on your health and confidence.

To ensure that you are proactively managing your mental and physical health, schedule the appointment you've been putting off as soon as possible—maybe you can even bolster your confidence immediately by scheduling an overdue check-up or finally looking for a new doctor that gives you more confident care. Being in control of your health is the #1 KCI and priority for managing a confident life.

## KCI #2: Education & Street Smarts

Being married to a 5th grade teacher and living next to an assistant superintendent, I'd be in deep doo-doo if I said formal education doesn't matter. It most certainly does for many reasons. However, your confidence doesn't depend on it.

There are so many examples of confident individuals who didn't go to Harvard or MIT—people who never even went to or graduated from college. These people are supremely confident. Steve Jobs, Mark Wahlberg, Bill Gates...those are the poster children. Do you even know or care what college George Clooney, Angelina Jolie or your own confidence role model went to?

In fact, in my own firsthand experiences with Ivy-educated individuals, I find an elite education often makes individuals less confident. Some of the smartest people are the least confident. Many are introverted and driven to learning for recreation or as an alternative to social interaction. Others are so competitive that they are just intimidated by other smart, driven individuals. Every college recognizes this and values well-rounded students who achieve more than just good grades in the classroom.

Colleges want kids who do sports, music, art, volunteer and work, because these kids are the kinds of candidates who are most likely more resilient and armed with important life skills such as teamwork, ability to deal with alone time, committed to practicing and can cope with failure, etc. In many ways, well-roundedness is the foreground of KCIs: buckets of things that keep our lives rich and balanced.

Let's get back to this specific KCI: education and street smarts. If you consider the goal of education to be knowledge, then the end game is having the information and experience needed to get and perform a job or task. You can learn some of this in a classroom or from a book, but obviously, much of life is taught via role models, mentors, trial and error and your own life story.

Let's go back to Mark Wahlberg (not just because I lust for him but because he's a great example here!) Marky Mark had a tough, criminal beginning and for many serendipitous reasons, he was able to rise above them and make himself into a respected actor, entrepreneur and seemingly great family role model. His intelligence isn't marked by his degrees or his eloquence but rather his resourcefulness a.k.a. street smarts. What I love about Mark beyond his muscles is that he is humble and acknowledges his past mistakes. He credits a lot of people and luck to his ability to take control and rise above—well above—the path that he was on to subsequently gain fame and fortune. Did it make him the man he is today? Certainly. Could he have done it by going to Yale instead? Who knows?

The reality is that getting a good education is like filling our mental tanks with gas so when we get into the "real world," we at least believe we have the knowledge to handle life, including professional pursuits.

To my teacher husband and all other educators that I gratefully respect, please keep teaching and pushing our kids and systems to make us smarter and more confident citizens. However, for all the achievement-driven parents who are stressed out trying to vicariously manage their kids' educational creds (I admit I often fall into this mindset trap, too), remember that confidence isn't determined by grades or degrees. Education is an important ingredient to feed our confidence and provides us with the skills, rules and directions about how certain games are played. However, a degree isn't the only way to learn, and it can be substituted or augmented with other things that give someone the knowledge and resourcefulness needed to win the ultimate prize of a confident and successful life.

### KCI #3: Financial Security & Control

We'd all like to have at least 'enough' money to live comfortably and have the option to retire when we want. Working against these goals, Western society seduces us to want more—more vacation time and choices, fancier cars, more luxurious homes, trendier gadgets, more fashionable clothes, etc. However, a 2010 Princeton University Woodrow Wilson School study[27] of American adults found that after an individual earns more than $75,000 annually, happiness doesn't increase, but stress does.

Having money can bolster confidence because it's an inherent reflection of our value in society. We typically assume that someone with more money is more valuable—that is, they are either luckier, work harder, or are otherwise more worthy than other people. We rarely appreciate the effort or stress caused by that person's status because it's hard to pity someone with the rewards that money can buy.

It also isn't uncommon to feel the need to keep up with the Jones' and everyone else in your neighborhood. I bet you know many people (maybe even you) who bought a house that was out of their budget or invested in something beyond their means. Though, you may not know that they are deeply saddled with debt and riddled with stress.

As a society, we are encouraged to buy and spend as a show of social value, and then when we can't afford it, our confidence is what pays. There is nothing that ruins more relationships and self-worth than money.

If you don't have control of your spending, or a strategy for saving, investing and/or financial goals, I do suggest you consider getting outside financial help, even if you only have little to manage. In fact, when you have precious little money, it may be the best time and reason to get help given you need to be that much more conservative and mindful. Starting sooner gives you more time to compound interest and knowledge so you can accrue more wealth and wisdom while ensuring that the limited amount you have is in control.

Your confidence isn't just a reflection of how much money you have but rather, how well you manage it. If you concretely know your cash flow and future projections, this directly feeds your confidence. Think about business. No one will want to invest or work somewhere if there isn't control of the finances. The same applies to the business of your life.

Say you want to go to Hawaii and you know that you will need a certain amount of money to get there. Having a financial plan to achieve that will give you the confidence ticket to get there. Or, if you conclude that it is not possible given the current way you earn and need to spend, you will be sad for sure. However, if you want to go to Hawaii badly enough, you will realize that you can proactively choose to make lifestyle changes. It may be ignorantly blissful to not recognize that you cannot currently afford to go to Hawaii. Down deep, in your core, you know that having real confidence, and not just hope, is all about having control and a plan. A financial plan gives you control over your money. So if you need a professional financial planner or investment advisor to get that control, then take control and do it. Sitting on the Hawaiian beach with frozen daiquiri in hand will be even sweeter when you think about your successful plan and the actions that made the trip possible.

How and who to select to get financial help is another story. I am not able to tell you the requirements as they should be based on your own needs and preferences. Certainly it is good advice to interview a few planners and get referrals from other people you respect that use planners. Most importantly, ask the candidates a lot of questions beyond the obvious things such as the methodology used and his/her historical track record. Listen for personal cues about the individual and their own values. Ask him or her how they manage their own money and time so you can see if it's aligned with your own values. Pick someone that you feel has both the skills and compassion to do the right thing for you, and is not just out for their commission. Liken it to a hairstylist. You don't want a hairstylist to cut your hair to look like their own! You want someone that is willing and able to cut your hair so it flatters your own face and lifestyle. A prospective financial partner(s) should prove to you in concrete ways that he or she can help you achieve your own financial goals. Don't give up until you find someone that really feels right. Once engaged, have them do a long-term, customized plan for you. You'll feel incredibly confident with that KCI bucket off your 'to do' list.

And *PLEASE*, compare your financial partner and investments with others in the market in terms of fees, results and responsiveness. If everyone else is losing money in the market, it's depressing but reassuring. Just don't close your eyes and let someone else steer your financial bus independently. Be an active passenger and with a well-vetted and somewhat supervised partner, you will then be able to drive in the direction that brings you financial confidence.

### KCI #4: Pastimes & Possessions

Go shop. You read me right. Go buy something! After I just told you to have financial control, I am now telling you to spend. However, here's the catch: buy something that you can afford and that brings you true pleasure.

It doesn't have to be expensive or even luxurious. It can be something small like an ice cream cone or iTunes song. It can be something practical but it must be something that makes you *feel* good—maybe some nice smelling hand cream or comfy socks. Or if you prefer, do something that is fun like a hobby or pastime. Go to a movie, build something or play a board game. Just make sure it's something you are doing simply for fun and not out of obligation. Golf doesn't count if you are networking or otherwise intentionally doing business on the course. Reading a book club selection counts—but only if it's something you really enjoy—and not just to avoid fellow reader wrath.

As a KCI, pastimes & possessions are important since they are the rewards of living. When we have the time and money to do and buy things 'just because we like them,' it is empowering and builds our confidence by validating our earned opportunity to simply have fun.

Buying a fancy sports car or shoes can count but, again, the rule is buy what you can afford and that truly brings you pleasure. If you are buying something to show off or attract attention, it's not going to truly bolster your core confidence. Only you can say what will ultimately bring personal pleasure and fulfillment. Therefore, take a moment to think about some of the things that you simply love to do or own and why—and what things you wish you did or owned and why not? Don't just make a bucket list—think about what's held you back thus far and why. The real aha moments come from recognizing you have legitimate reasons for doing or not doing those things.

Too busy with kids? Work sucks up all your time? Can't fit in time even to exercise, let alone do something for fun? Yeah—you know those are all common but perhaps telling excuses. It is certainly important to consider your priorities and why they are priorities. However, have you ever considered the implications of not doing something? In business, we call these opportunity costs. If you don't do something for yourself, how does that weigh on your confidence and happiness? Can you be a great parent or employee if you deprive yourself? Remember all work and no play makes Jack a very dull boy.[28] Turns out it makes him a frustrated, stressed and all together insecure individual, too.

So now you have not just permission but an excuse to go buy some hot shoes or get a hot stone massage. Just promise yourself it's something you can afford, and that it will make you feel really good just because you truly enjoy it.

### KCI #5: Outer Beauty & Personal Care

Another myth busted: beauty doesn't only come from within. Your *OUTSIDE* looks actually impact how you feel *INSIDE*—and vice versa. Think about the last time you got a haircut, a manicure or other grooming treatment. Most likely, you left feeling more confident. You walked a little taller, felt a little sexier and knew you were taking care of YOU.

It may seem like superficial confidence but consider that if something makes you feel more attractive on the outside, it will bolster your confidence on the inside. Remember the discussion before on the "look of confidence?" It's often not the best-looking person that looks the best. It's the one who projects confidence and implies "I do look good." When you make the effort to do your hair or shave carefully, it's a confidence badge earned.

What about a bad hair day or exposed zit? These are definitely potential confidence busters, but by adopting a more confident attitude, you'll realize that these temporary blemishes aren't nearly as noticeable to other people— seriously! Or if they are, consider why you care. Someone who is judging you for your hair may or may not be important to you. Maybe their judgment of you can function as simple feedback—that you should have spent more effort to fix the issue (hair, pimple, etc.). Yes, it is easy to say and write but the reality is that everyone has a bad hair or face day. Everyone wishes sometimes that they had more time or money to look like a celebrity—even celebrities. But, if you put out a confident vibe, people will notice that well before a transient pimple.

Study after study confirms that people who think they are attractive are perceived by others to be attractive, even if in reality they aren't. Many of these studies also note that such people have higher self-esteem and tend to take better care of themselves.

> *"Thus, happy people appear not only to do more to enhance their appearance, but they also perceive themselves as more attractive compared with less happy individuals."*
>
> Excerpted from: "Physical Attractiveness and
> Subjective Well-Being"
> Diener, E., Wolsic, B. and Fujita, F.[30]

Regardless of which is the cause and which is the effect, the result is that you can be as beautiful as you feel, no matter how you look. Confidence is your best accessory!

### KCI #6: Sleep & Think Time

I love Arianna Huffington for many reasons, especially since she's as firm of a supporter of getting a good night's sleep as my expensive mattress! Intuitively, it seems obvious that when we are tired, we have less patience, less focus and less control of our words and actions. Turns out, exhaustion weakens our confidence, too.

In Arianna's book, *Thrive,* [31] she refers to a study published in *Science* that determined that an extra hour of sleep can do more for daily happiness than a $60,000 raise!

It is unavoidably hard to focus if you are tired. You simply can't think productively when you are tired and bombarded with social noise and distraction. Even when we attempt to focus, we can't help but allow our thoughts to be overtaken by distraction. When was the last time you focused on driving somewhere in silence rather than talking on the phone or listening to a book on tape?

Do you make any concerted time to just think and not "do?"

> *"In a rushed, harried, stressed-out state, the onslaught of what we have to do can go by in a jumbled blur. But rested and focused, what's coming next appears to slow down, allowing us to manage it with calm and confidence. "*
>
> Arianna Huffington, in her book *Thrive* [31]

Meditation, yoga, deep breathing, visualization, and dozens of other techniques are used to lasso our brain noise into submissive silence. Praying, chanting, and for some people, listening to music, are ways to unplug from the outside world and tune into the one in your own head. Talk to anyone that meditates and they say confidently it's the best part of his or her day. *Parade's* January 11, 2015 issue touted mediation as the #1 health booster, noting superstars like Oprah, Ellen and Paul McCartney are advocates. So, even if your bathroom stall doesn't offer you a formal class in mindfulness (like the ones I mentioned in the beginning at Cambridge Innovation Center), you can still try to take a few extra minutes while you are tinkling to do some thinking!

Maybe an even easier thing to do is to mindfully notice when you are tired and haven't had the time or ability to think. By acknowledging that you are pooped or scatter-brained, you may be able to hold back on saying or doing something you will later regret. You will recognize you aren't able to operate at peak performance and may even postpone (if possible) things that require your focus and control. Elite athletes have strict sleep schedules to ensure they rest both their minds and bodies. We implicitly know a good night's rest is invaluable to performing well on tests. While we zip around all day running and multitasking, we forget how important sleep and thinking are to feeding our mental and physical engines.

Did you know that falling asleep at the wheel kills more people than alcohol or other factors? I bet being tired is also the leading killer of careers, relationships and personal achievements. Like a drunk driver, when you are tired, you can easily lose control of your car and confidence.

With minimal effort, you can recognize when you are tired and, hopefully now, you will put more effort into biting your tongue or just deferring action until you are better rested. Use your exhaustion as an excuse to temporarily bow out of a confrontation or something that requires positive energy until you can bring your best. As Arianna says, "Sleep your way to the top!"—top of your game, that is!

### KCI #7: Faith & Protection

Having faith is one of the big attributes that differentiates us from the rest of the animal kingdom (at least from what the animals have shared with us!) Our sense of hope and optimism is a survival skill that allows us to take on the slings and arrows of life. Whether we have religion guiding our faith or just a general appreciation that life happens, faith is a comfort. In many ways, it protects us from the dark side of thinking that could make us depressed and/or act in socially unacceptable ways. Faith is, in many senses, a protection of our own psyche as well as a way to control or at least buffer us from the actions of others. You may not think that golden lessons like "Do unto others" and "Love thy brother" are forms of protection, but they formulate most of our laws that allow us to live in harmony. Legal systems and beliefs give us an underlying social contract providing faith and confidence that we are respected by and not normally harmed by our brethren.

Unfortunately, in today's world, religions and laws aren't powerful enough to guarantee our safety. Individuals own personal weapons and other means of protecting themselves from physical, financial, social and other potential harm. You actually can feel protected from things such as dogs, insurance policies, alarms and even your own muscles.

Reducing our vulnerability to one of these potential harms is like knowing how to block or throw a karate kick. We want to be prepared and able to defend ourselves so we aren't compromised or worse, have to experience loss. We actively seek ways to minimize the chances of experiencing harm, and plan for contingencies so we can recover as fast and easily as possible. With these types of policies and plans in place, we actually gain confidence. We know we can't control a tornado from leveling our house, but we can strengthen our confidence by being protected in case we need to rebuild.

It's pretty straightforward to identify things that should be protected: your home, car, business, children, income, pet, jewelry and other valuable people and possessions. Take 10 minutes to take stock of these things and consider if they are protected now and in the future. It may bring up some scary thoughts but this is important to do while it is hypothetical. Only then can you rationally put plans in place to ensure you have confident protection. It's typically uncomfortable to talk about death or disability but it is also empowering once you put a plan in place to deal with it. Think of planning for the worst as similar to carrying an umbrella. We often joke that it won't rain when we carry an umbrella around all day. But if it does rain, we are truly glad to have that umbrella ready to protect our heads and bodies. And no, that is not what is meant by umbrella insurance!

Just like with financial security and control, getting trusted advisors to help you know how and how much protection you want to have (not just want you are required to have) can be a valuable exercise. You can insure everything you own and do, but that is not very practical. Plus, insurance isn't the only way to protect what you love. Proper maintenance and storage is also important for possessions. Being a caring individual helps protect those you love. First, inventory what you want to protect and then get trusted, expert advice on how to protect it best. To fill this KCI bucket, take some time to think. Gathering information and acting in accordance with what you value (literally) will ensure that you are can be confident that you are doing what is needed to protect those things.

## KCI #8: Human Support & Connections

Abraham Maslow's Hierarchy of Needs[1] still is a fundamental part of modern psychology theory and practice. It explains psychological elements that feed our motivations to behave and express ourselves in socially desirable ways. It is perhaps obvious, that our need for food, shelter and safety must be fulfilled before we can love, and that our ability to love feeds our self-esteem and freedom to be creative. However, it is perhaps more evident today than before that the middle of the hierarchy is where many people get stuck—the need to belong and be loved.

'Belonging' provides us with personal purpose and fit. Without this, Maslow argues that that if we don't feel we belong, we cannot fully gain esteem in ourselves (or others). Nor can we reach our full potential as expressive, compassionate individuals. Humans (like most animals) find belonging through family and friends. We also seek belonging through clubs, religious organizations, professional associations, workplaces, sororities/fraternities and even in bars ("where everybody knows your name..."[32]). The comfort of being in a welcoming environment gives you place and purpose, familiarity and acceptance.

Whether we are young or old, the need to belong is critical to our wellbeing. However, people need different levels of belonging. Some people need more constant contact with others to feel connected. Other people find occasional meetings enough.

A recent Microsoft study[33], commissioned by Dove, found that social media is clearly impacting the way women perceive their own and other people's confidence. Principal researcher danah boyd *(intentionally not capitalized per individual's preference)* commented, "Social media is playing a critical role in showing and shaping how women and girls feel about themselves." Yet, women do not realize how online dialogue can contribute to negative mindsets and behavior towards beauty both on and offline. In a future ACI research study, I hope to explore the impact of social media on our overall need to belong. I believe that social media both helps and hurts us. Subsequently, if not well understood and managed, social media will undoubtedly create a void of true social connectivity and sense of belonging. For example, it is no secret that people usually post only "the good stuff." Yet, we easily fall into the trap of thinking other people have a better life, more friends and are having more fun than we are. We measure self-worth by the number of friends, connections and likes that we have—and we are impressed by others that have many. We forget that making a Facebook friend is easy and not very risky. Our social media profiles also portray only what we want other people to see and know—and to some extent, our perceived profiles are editable.

> *"There is evidence that it (social media) can begin to actually rewire our brains to make us less adept at real human connection."*
>
> Arianna Huffington, *Thrive*

In my book, *Ms. Informed: Wake Up Wisdom for Women*, one of the most popular chapters is about friends. I segment friends into three groups. Some are 911 friends that you can 'call with any emergency' type of friends. I compare them to 711 friends who are 'friends of convenience' (named after 7-Eleven convenience stores). I note that from the research I did as part of *Ms. Informed*, most people have one or two 911 friends and dozens of 711 friends—especially when we are young or when are in the stage where it "takes a village to help raise children." The research shows that as people age, 711 friends wane. The reason is most likely that as we age, we learn that it is more fulfilling to have a few deep relationships than lots of superficial ones. We also learn that spending time with people you really don't enjoy being with isn't worthwhile, and we finally have the confidence not to! This is all part of our maturation and increased wisdom. Something that made me laugh once was an audience member saying that social media friends are like 411—the kind you'd look up in the white pages. They may be great for a quick chat or question but most likely, they won't come running if you need them to mind your kids or take care of you when you are sick.

Millennials have dramatically different resources, expectations and connections than the prior generations. Their ways of belonging are seemingly different, too. Thus, as time passes it will be interesting to see how online interaction impacts the overall human hierarchy of needs.

Meanwhile, you can assess your connection and points of belonging. Don't measure your net worth by the size of your network. Consider your 911 friends and family members those that really keep you rooted and who genuinely root for you. Consider other ways you can find connection through organizations or online. Realize the importance of those connections beyond the potential opportunities they might bring. And, appreciate that those connections are filling a critical need right now: they help you belong to something which in turn, raises you through Maslow's hierarchy towards becoming who you really want to and can be.

What about kids? Can we impact our kids' confidence? Do they impact our own? Whether you are a parent or not, you are most likely a relative, friend or teacher and therefore, you have surely impacted a child's confidence at some point. While there are hundreds of books and experts on this very subject, I won't expound here. In the context of confidence, you can plant seeds of confidence by understanding and adapting your own rearing decisions by not confusing confidence with imposters or confidence cousins that were discussed previously in this book. With a better understanding of what confidence is and is not, you can become more confident of what guides and educates others, especially children.

The easiest way to do this is to become the inspirational medium or "soil" that grows confidence by being a confidence mentor and model. By modeling confident self-management you can help germinate the seeds of confidence in others, young and old, who will, in turn, become stronger and more resilient. The process and result will pay it back to you since you helped create another confident individual. That is an uber-confident contribution and is possibly the best way you can give and get your own dose of KCI #8.

# Assessing & Addressing Confidence

Now that you understand and hopefully appreciate the importance of each KCI, you can quickly build a structure to help visualize these using a **Personal Confidence Dashboard.**

The next steps are simple: use the Personal Confidence Dashboard below. It asks you the same 5 questions for each KCI to help assess where your key confidence indicators are right now relative to how important each KCI is to you (and your values).

There are no right or wrong answers, and your answers will likely change over time. The objective is to see the confidence 'buckets' that are filled appropriately, and those that need some attention. You can revisit this tool every day or every week as KCIs rating shifts constantly. However, after you do this once, you will be able to better identify and address confidence indicators automatically. Think of this as a life machine with dials that you can adjust to proactively manage your own confidence.

Once you fill in your Personal Confidence Dashboard, you will see the areas that are in good shape versus the ones that require your attention. To address the weaker KCIs, the process will then guide you through a few simple questions that create a plan of specific action. We even give you some starter ideas in Appendix 1.

Just putting a plan in place will raise your confidence. Then when you achieve your confidence plan, you'll get a major confidence boost and the enthusiasm to tackle other areas— or maybe even help someone else tackle their's.

# Personal Confidence Dashboard

Ask yourself these questions for each Key Confidence Indicator (KCI). For each question you answer 'Yes,' give yourself one point in that KCI. Color in your point totals below to get a visual observation of your current overall core confidence.

1. Can you justify the time and money you spend (or don't spend) on this?
2. Do you feel in control of this KCI more than 75% of the time?
3. Do you take deliberate action to improve this KCI every week?
4. Do you have realistic examples that accurately measure your level in this KCI?
5. Do you have a response mechanism to take action when this KCI is stressed?

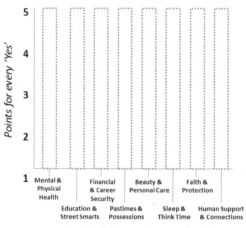

*Key Confidence Indicators (KCIs)*

@2015 American Confidence Institute
www.AmericanConfidenceInstitute.com

Kickass Confidence: Assessing & Addressing Confidence

A completed Personal Confidence Dashboard might look something like this:

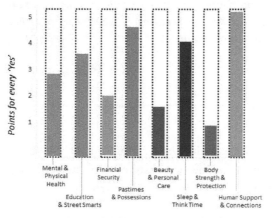

*Key Confidence Indicators (KCIs)*

It's easy to see that this person's area of confidence needing the most immediate attention is Body Strength and Protection. Now this individual can focus and address this area with a tactical plan of action.

*"No one can make you feel inferior without your consent."*

Eleanor Roosevelt

# Personal Confidence Plan

> *"Confidence is something we can, to a significant extent, control. We can all make a decision, at any point in our lives, to create more of it."*
>
> Kay and Shipman, *The Confidence Code*

Now, look at your own resulting Personal Confidence Dashboard. Answer the following questions to create a practical and Personal Confidence Plan using small win actions.

1. Referring to your Personal Confidence Dashboard, which are your high KCIs?

2. Which KCIs are low?

3. Pick one low KCI that you'd like to focus on first. Why did you pick that KCI?

4. What is one thing you will commit to yourself to do immediately to improve that KCI? (See Appendix 1 for ideas!)

5. How will you know your plan is working?

Once you get that KCI in better shape, you can move on to another KCI. Unlike physical fitness training, it's much harder to condition multiple confidence areas simultaneously. Tackling one is empowering and will help you tackle subsequent ones. You may even need to go back to a previously addressed KCI and kick it up again, maybe in a different way. For example, if your Human Support & Connections KCI is weak, you might throw a party or go out with some friends. Weeks later, you may find it low again and need to join a new club or go to someone else's party!

Many people enjoy working with a life coach as a thought partner to go through the initial assessment and plan. A life or executive coach can also be really helpful after you build a Personal Confidence Dashboard as a source of accountability and support. Yet other people may require clinical help to really cull out more traumatic and causal issues.

The Personal Confidence Dashboard provides a simple structure and results in a visual format that anyone can interpret. After one or two times using the dashboard, most people report they maintain a memorized checklist that helps them constantly evaluate their confidence levels—almost subconsciously—so that they can make better decisions and feel guided in their actions. The dashboard helps them remember priorities and deflect other people's bonehead behavior.

KCIs aren't a cure-all but rather a way to help many of us as we are run around trying to multitask like chickens with their confident heads cut off. KCIs helps us remember to take mindful breaths and use our bigger-than-birdbrains to simply take stock. Just knowing that you can take control of your KCI buckets, helps build core confidence.

> *"And every day, the world will drag you by the hand, yelling, 'This is important! And this is important! And this is important! You need to worry about this! And this! And this! ...And every day, it's up to you to yank your hand back, put it on your heart and say, 'No. This is what's important.'"*
>
> Iain Thomas as excerpted from Arianna Huffington's *Thrive*

# Confident Conclusions

Confidence is the frame for what we allow ourselves to do and believe. Our own confidence directs other people as to how they should judge us and how we should interact with each other. More than a predetermined or implicit pecking order, confidence dictates what we dream of doing, how we dare to behave and what we insist on being known for.

More subconsciously, confidence is required to get into the zone, to manage stress and to find balance between one's own head, heart and heels. It is a welcomed whisper to challenge what we think is not possible, and it is the medicine we use to salve wounds of rejection. Unfortunately, when our confidence is shot, it is not easily sewn up. Yet, when we have strong core confidence, we tend to recover faster and even stronger than before.

My genie-granted wish would be that I could have known about confidence sooner. Though not regretfully, it is interesting to consider how having more confidence might have changed how I chose my career, my friends, and even how I live. It certainly would have made being a parent and dealing with Zak's dystonia easier. I still would have been freaked out, but at least I would have realized sooner that doctors have their limitations like the rest of us.

I know now that there was an invisible but clear path for me— from being a motivated, Maslovian marketer to writing *Ms. Informed* and thus meeting Lynnette. Lynnette opened my mind to neuroplasticity and provided the comfortable opportunity to come to Toronto so we could explore together how to clinically improve confidence. It was only for this reason that I came to understand neuroplasticity and how it is being used to improve athletic performance. Our trip to Toronto would explore these technologies and techniques to see if they could possibly help ACI clients and maybe even Zak—at least with upping his tennis game. With the trip booked months in advance, it was an email that I received three weeks prior to our trip that was the ultimate kicker. The email was from the author of a book I had downloaded three years prior. The book was about dystonia and while available only as a PDF, I had struggled to read only part of it due to the unusual case study style in which it was written and my inability to understand the author's medical comments regarding the case study treatments and results. The PDF remained on my computer desktop, unread and occasionally tempting me to delete it. Therefore, what caught my attention in the email was that the author, Dr. Farias, noted that he had moved from Spain to Toronto to see patients who wanted to use movement therapy (neuroplasticity) rather than more invasive dystonia treatments. It was a bizarre coincidence or maybe a divine intervention that I couldn't believe. He was doing exactly what I was thinking was possible: retraining the brain, in this case, to overcome dystonia. We scheduled time to see Dr. Farias on our trip and 30 minutes after meeting him, we witnessed the miracle of Zak's recovery.

Finding Dr. Farias was the ultimate prize—better than winning the lottery. But, in the end, I wouldn't have found him had it not been for my confidence crusade that left little me—a mom and marketer—convinced that she could find a potential cure for something as complex as a neurological condition like focal dystonia.

I now know that confidence is the true secret and source of every decision and action we make. It is the fuel we use to navigate life with all its rewards and challenges. Confidence allows us to be who we want and find happiness in what we gain and give to the world.

Therefore, this book and its topic of confidence is the legacy I hope to leave for my own universe. My hope is that you will also want to practice and impart the power of confidence to those you impact.

> *"People will forget what you said, people will forget what you did, but people will never forget how you made them feel."*
>
> Maya Angelou

We live in a world that is information rich and subsequently confidence poor. With social media, plus the onslaught of global competition, our confidence is being challenged in new ways that require new support modalities. And as researchers continue to delve deeper into technology to help understand and control the brain, more questions are being raised than can possibly answered.

Clearly, a lot more research and discussion is needed to understand how and why we are confident, and how we can build confidence that is automatic and sustainable. This research needs to include more than a single discipline, and therefore requires new ways of funding and collaborating. Politics and profit will continue to largely direct what and how research is funded. Plus, beyond the money, we need scientists who are willing to take risks by defending their own educated beliefs and credentials in pursuit of answers that may not be all initially academically organized or departmentally bounded. Yes, we need core confident scientists!

Confidence cuts across all people and conditions. It may be a root cause or a desired result of all human behavior. It is both desired and feared. Therefore, it does not fit into a clear charitable space that pulls at donor heartstrings or personal endorsement opportunities. But please allow me to think like John Lennon just for a moment and imagine—imagine a world of confident individuals. How would this impact everything—from our laws to wars? Would we all grow up more capable and motivated? Would we stress out as much about our kids or our own well-being? Would we need as much medication or therapy?

Pardon my infringement, John. Today, I think we need more than love—in the end, I think all we really need is confidence.

> *"There's nowhere you can be that*
> *isn't where you're meant to be.*
> *It's easy."*
>
> John Lennon and Paul McCartney

# Bibliography

## Footnotes

[1] Abraham Maslow – good listing of resources to learn about the inventor of "The Hierarchy of Needs" http://www.maslow.com/.

[2] Goldie Hawn's MindUP classroom programs to teach mindfulness: http://thehawnfoundation.org/mindup/.

[3] Lumosity's neuroscience based games. http://www.lumosity.com/.

[4] "Do Cool Sh*t!" book: http://www.amazon.com/Do-Cool-Sh-Business-Happily/dp/0062261533.

[5] Nike's well-known tagline. www.Nike.com.

[6] "The Confidence Code" book and other info: http://theconfidencecode.com/.

[7] Info about what are and how to do Kegels - http://www.mayoclinic.org/healthy-lifestyle/womens-health/in-depth/kegel-exercises/art-20045283.

[8] "Sexy and I know it" are title and lyrics of a popular 2011 LMFAO song.

[9] Brewer, B. W., Van Raalte, J. L., Linder, D. E., & Van Raalte, N. S.. "Peak performance and the perils of retrospective introspection." Sept 1991, *Journal of Sport & Exercise Psychology*, Vol. 13, No. 3, pp 227-238.

[10] Myers-Briggs tests and other personality assessments: http://www.myersbriggs.org/.

[11] PI score developed and property of http://www.piworldwide.com/.

[12] www.Dictionary.com definition of self-esteem.

[13] Dove's Self-esteem campaign, http://www.dove.us/Our-Mission/Girls-Self-Esteem/default.aspx.

[14] L'Oreal's "Because You're Worth It" campaign, http://www.lorealparisusa.com/en/about-loreal-paris/because-youre-worth-it.aspx.

[15] Baumeister, R.F., Campbell, J.D. Krueger, J.I, & Vohs, K.D., "Does self-esteem cause better performance, interpersonal success, happiness, or healthier lifestyles? 2003, *Psychological Science in the Public Interest*, Vol. 4, No. 1, pgs 4, 1-44.

[16] The movie, *The Wizard of Oz,* 1939 Warner Bros.

[17] Carol Dweck, "*Growth Mindset*", http://mindsetonline.com/abouttheauthor/.

[18] Brooks, R., "The Power to Change Your Life: Ten Keys to Resilient Living" http://www.drrobertbrooks.com/wp/wp-content/uploads/2003/10/The-Power-to-Change-Your-Life-Ten-Keys-to-Resilient-Living.pdf.

[19] Haynes, S., "Is Self Compassion More Important Than Self Esteem?" http://www.huffingtonpost.com/steven-c-hayes-phd/is-selfcompassion-more-im_b_6316320.html.

[20] "Henry VIII", by William Shakespeare.

[21] Norton, M. & Gino, F., "Why Rituals Work" , http://www.scientificamerican.com/article/why-rituals-work/.

[22] Diener, R., "The Courage Quotient: How Science Can Make You Braver" http://intentionalhappiness.com/.

[23] Chambliss,D., "Champions: The Making of Olympic Swimmers", http://www.amazon.com/Champions-The-Making-Olympic-Swimmers/dp/0688076181.

[24] Tugade, M. & Fredrickson, B., "Regulation of Positive emotions: Emotion Regulation Strategies that promote resilience." *Journal of Happiness Studies*, 2007, pp. 311-333.

[25] Kiani, R. & Shadlen, M.N.. "Representation of confidence associated with a decision by neurons in the parietal cortex." 2009, *Science 324*, pp 759-764.

[26] "Outliers", Malcolm Gladwell http://gladwell.com/outliers/the-10000-hour-rule/

[27] Hebart, M.N, Schriever, Y., Donner, T.H., & Haynes, J-D., "The relationship between perceptual decision variables and confidence in the human brain." 2014, Oxford University Press, http://www.tobiasdonner.eu/publications/hebartCC2014.pdf

[28] 2010 Princeton University Woodrow Wilson School study http://wws.princeton.edu/news-and-events/news/item/two-wws-professors-release-new-study-income%E2%80%99s-influence-happiness

[29] Quote from the movie "The Shining". 1980 Warner Bros.

[30] Diener, E., Wolsic, B, & Fujita, F., "Physical Attractiveness and Subjective Well-Being." 1995, *Journal of Personality and Social Psychology*, pp. 69, 120-129.

[31] Huffington, A., "Thrive", http://thrive.huffingtonpost.com/

[32] From the Cheers show theme song, http://en.wikipedia.org/wiki/Where_Everybody_Knows_Your_Name

[33] Microsoft study commissioned by Dove
http://www.multivu.com/players/English/7447351-dove-twitter-speak-beautiful/

**Additional Sources of information:**

Abbruzzese, G., Trompetto, C., Mori, L, and Pelosin, E. "Rehabilitation of upper limb dysfunction in movement disorders: a clinical perspective." *Frontiers in Human Neuroscience*, Nov. 2014, Vol. 8, Article 961.

Bachkirova, T. "Dealing with issues of the self-concept and self-improvement strategies in coaching and mentoring." 2004, *International Journal of Evidence Based Coaching and Mentoring*, Vol. 2, No. 2, pp 29-40.

http://www.beckyblalock.com/

Brooks, R. "Ten Keys to Resilient Living." 2003, www.drrobertsbrooks.com.

Carver, C.S., Scheier, M.F., Weinstraub, J.K., "Assessing Coping Strategies: A Theoretically Based Approach." *Journal of Personality and Social Psychology*, 1989, Vol. 56, No. 2,pp 267-283.

Cohn, M.A., Fredrickson, B.L., Brown, S. Mikels, J.A., and Conway, A. M., "Happiness Unpacked: Positive Emotions Increase Life Satisfaction By Building Resilience." 2009, *Emotion*, Vol. 9, No. 3, pp 361-368.

Crabb, S. "The use of coaching principles to foster employee engagement." *The Coaching Psychologist*, Vol. 7, No. 1, pp 27-34.

Crocker, J. & Park, L. "The costly pursuit of self-esteem." 2004, *Psychological Bulletin*, pp 130, 392-414.

Dawes, R.M. "Confidence in intellectual judgements vs. confidence in perceptual judgements." 1980.

De Martino, B., Fleming, S.M., Garrett, N. & Dolan, R. "Confidence in value-based choice." Jan 2013, *National Neuroscience,* pp 16, 105-110.

Diener, Ed & Biswas-Diener, R. "Will money increase subjective well-being?" 2002, Social Indictors Research, pp 57, 119-169.

Diener, Ed, Wolsic, Brian and Fujita, Frank, "Physical Attractiveness and Subjective Well-Being." *Journal of Personality and Social Psychology,* 1995, Vol. 69, No. 1, pp 120-129.

Di Paula, A. & Campbell, J.D. "Self-esteem and persistence in the face of failure." *Journal of Personality and Social Psychology,* 2002, pp 83, 711-724.

Gariepy, J-F., "Prefrontal brain areas rtack subjective confidence." Dec. 14, 2012. BrainFacts.org.

Greenberg, J. Solomon, S., Pyszczynski, T. Rosenblatt, A., Burling, J., Lyon, D., et al. "Why do people need self-esteem? Converging evidence that self-esteem serves as an anxiety-buffering function." 1999.

Halvorson, H. G. "To Succeed, Forget Self-Esteem." Sep 2012, *Lifehacker.com.*

Hatfield, E., & Sprecher, S. "Mirror, Mirror: The importance of looks in everyday life." 1986.

Hayes, S. "Is Self-Compassion more Important Than elf-Esteem?" 12/17/2014, huffingtonPost.com.

Heffernan, M., *A Bigger Prize,* 2014.

Henderson, J.M., "Is Social Media Destroying Your Self Esteem?" Nov. 2012, *Forbes.*

Insabato, A., Pannunzi, M., Rolls, E.T., Deco, G. "Confidence-Related Decision Making." July 2010, *Journal of Neurophysiology*, pp 104, 539-547.

Judge, T.A., & Hurst, C. "Capitalizing on one's advantages: Role of core self-evaluations." 2007, *Journal of Applied Psychology*, pp 92, 1212-1227.

Judge, T.A., Hurst, C, & Simon, Lauren S., "Does It Pay to Be Smart, Attractive, or Confidence (or All Three)? Relationships Among General Mental Ability, Physical Attractiveness, Core self-Evaluations, and Income." 2009, *Journal of Applied Psychology*, Vol 92, No. 3 pp 3, 742-755.

Judge, T.A., & Hurst, C. "How the Rich (and Happy) Get Richer (and Happier): Relationship of Core Self-Evaulaitions to trajectories in Attaining Work Success" 2008, *Journal of Applied Psychology*, Vol 93, No. 4, pgs 849-863.

Judge, T.A. & Bono J.E, "Relationship of Core Self-Evaluations Traits—Self-Esteem, Generalized Self-Efficacy, Locus of Control, and Emotional Stability—With Job Satisfaction and Job Performance: A Meta-Analysis." 2001, *Journal of Applied Psychology*, Vol. 86, No. 1, pp 80-92.

Kalyman, J., Soll, J.B., Barlas, S. "Overconfidence: It Depends on How, What, and Whom You Ask." 1999, *Organizational Behavior and Human Decision Processes*, Vol 79, No. 3, pp 216-247.

Kanai, R., Dong, M.Y., Bahrami, N. & Rees, G. "Distractibility in Daily Life is Reflected in the Structure and Function of Human Parietal Cortex." May 4, 2011, *The Journal of Neuroscience*, pp 6620-6626.

Kepecs, A., Mainen, Z. "A computational framework or the study of confidence in humans and animals." 2012, Royal Society Publishing.

Kluger, Jeffrey. "Get Your Head In the Game." February 23-March 2, 2015, *Time, pp* 83-86.

Kuster, F., Orth, U., & Meier, L.L., "High Self-Esteem Prospectively Predicts Better Work Conditions and Outcomes.", *Social Psychological and Personality Science*, Vol. 4 No. 6, pp 668-675.

Lau, H. & Rosenthal, D., "Empirical support for higher-order theories of conscious awareness." August 2011, *Trends in Cognitive Sciences,* Vol. 15, No. 8, pp 365-373.

www.MindTools.com

Mobias, M.M. & Rosenblatt, T.S. "Why beauty matters." 2006, *American Economic Review*, pp 96, 222-235.

Murray, S.L. Holmes, J.G., & Griffin, D.W. "Self-esteem and the quest for felt security: How perceived regard regulates attachment processes." 2000, *Journal of Personality and Social Psychology,* pp 78, 478-498.

Newell, E. "Understanding Confidence in Sport" http://www.thesportinmind.com/articles/understanding-confidence-in-sport/

Neiss, N.B., Sedikides, C., & Stevenson, J. "Genetic influences on level and stability of self-esteem." 2006, *Self and Identity*, pp 5, 247-266.

Owler, K. "Facilitating Internal Motivation: Impacts of the Life Code Matrix Model on Working Life." Aug 2012, *International Journal of Evidence Based Coaching and Mentoring*, Vol. 10, No. 2 pp 65-75.

Pickert, K., "The Mindful Revolution", Jan 23, 2014, *Time.*

Pink, D. H., *Drive.* 2009, Riverhead Books, Penguin.

Pleskac, Timothy J., Busemeyer, Jerome R., "Two Stage Dynamic Signal Detection: A Theory of Choice, Decision Time, and Confidence." 2010, *Psychological Review*, Vol. 117, No.3 pp 864-901.

Quartarone, A., Rizzo, V., Terranova, C., Milardi, D, Brushetta, D., Ghilardi, M.F. and Birlanda, P. "Sensory abnormalities in focal hand dystonia and non-invasive brain stimulation." Dec 2014, *Frontiers in Human Neuroscience*, Vol. 8, article 956.

Rando, C., "How to Overcome a Confidence Crisis." *www.selfgrowth.com.*

Rolls, E.T., Grabenhorst, F., & Deco G. "Decision-Making, Errors, and Confidence in the Brain." 2010, *Journal of Neurophysiology*, Vol. 104, pp 2359-2374.

Rolls, E.T., Grabenhorst, F., & Deco G."Choice, difficulty and confidence in the brain." 2010, *Neuroimage*, pp 53, 694-706.

Swann Jr., W.B., Chang-Schneider, C., & McClarty, K.L. "Yes, Cavalier Attitudes Can have Pernicious Consequences." 2008, *American Psychologist*, pp 65-66.

Swann Jr., W.B., Chang-Schneider, C., & McClarty, K.L. , "Do People's Self-Views Matter?  Self-Concept and Self-Esteem in Everyday Life." February–March 2007, *American Psychologist*, Vol. 62, No. 2, 84–94.

Telegraph MEdia Group, UK December 18, 2014, "Social media blamed for crisis of confidence in British schoolgirls."

Trzesniewski, Kali H., Donellan, M. Brent, and Robins, Richard W. "Stability of Self-Esteem Across Life Span." 2003, *Journal of Personality and Social Psychology, Vol. 84, No. 1*, pp 205-220.

Tugade, M.M. & Fredrickson, B.L., "Regulation of Positive Emotions: Emotion Regulation Strategies That promote Resilience." 2007, *Journal of Happiness Studies*, pp 311-327.

Tugade, M.M. & Fredrickson, B.L. "Resilient individuals use positive emotions to bounce back from negative emotional experiences." 2004, *Journal of Personality and Social Psychology*, pp 86, 320-333.

Wells, G., "Peak Performance: A literature review." http://drgregwells.com/superbodies/

Woodard, C.R. "Hardiness and the concept of courage." 2004, *Consulting Psychology Journal: Practice and Research*, Vol. 56, No. 3, pp 173-185.

Young, J.A., Pain, M. D. "The Zone: Evidence of a Universal Phenomenon for Athletes." 1999, *Athletic Insight.*

Young, J.A., "In the zone" May 1999, *Tennis*, pp 40-41.

Zebrowitz, L.A., Collins, M.A., Dutta, R. "The relationship between appearance and personality across the life span." *Personality and Social Psychology*, pp 24, 736-749.

Zylberberg, A., Barttfeld, P. & Sigman, M. "The construction of confidence in perceptual decision." Sep 2012, *Frontiers in Integrative Neuroscience*, Vol 6, Article 79.

Zeigler-Hill, V. Clark, C.B. & Beckman, T.E. "Fragile self-esteem and the interpersonal circumflex: Are feelings of self-worth associated with interpersonal style?" 2011, *Self and Identity*, pp 10, 509-536.

Zeigler-Hill, Virgil, Holden, Christopher J., Enjaian, Brian, Southard, Ashton, Besseram Avi, Li, Haijiang, and Zhang, Qinglin, "Self-Esteem Instability and Personality: The Connections Between Feelings of Self-Worth and the Big Five Dimensions of Personality." 2015, *Personality and Social Psychology Bulletin*, Vol. 41, pp 183-198.

# Acknowledgements

Birthing a book is an emotional, humbling and scary process that takes not so much someone who is confident, but more like someone with unique luck. I am definitely one of the luckiest people on the planet having such wonderful friends and colleagues. I'd like to recognize some who helped specifically with this project. Your contributions of time, patience and knowledge cannot be completely thanked here, so these acknowledgements are only a bookmark to a future, in-person chapter when I get to thank you more profoundly.

To my ACI partner and the most thoughtful, fun and helpful person I ever met, Lynnette Rumble: I am not only honored by your choice in taking me on as a friend and colleague, but I am utterly inspired by your grace as a mother, coach and all things woman. Thank you to whoever/whatever allowed our paths to cross, and for giving us both the wisdom to know we needed to confide in one another.

My other great find and fortune is my husband who has not only the patience, but the stamina to put up with my being. Your support during this book process and all things we continue to tackle together are simply the reason I can and do.

I certainly attribute much of my inspiration to my kids, Ben and Zak. You both have such beautifully filled hearts and heads, that my greatest blessing is to be in *your* presence.

My aunt, Laurie Margolies, has always been a key source of my confidence—in trust and mentorship. Thank you for always being there—for listening and helping despite your own situation and needs. Your help with this book and all the things you do for me are completely appreciated.

I wouldn't be able to do much of anything, let alone this work without the candor and confidence of my mom, Nancy Cohen and sister, Jennifer Tuttelman. My sadly deceased grandparents Bert and Mort Margolies undoubtedly shaped my own confidence with 2 parts charisma and 1 part chutzpah.

Thank you for your unconditional support and appreciated friendship: Alison Martin-Books, Sharon Goldstein, Joy Levin, Kristin Deegan, Christa Degnan Manning, Tom Condardo, Marco Emrich, Lina Taylor, Jane Zupan and Lori Siragusa. To my kickass marketing and wine buddy, Jen McNeil, for blurting out the title one night. Shout out to Mei-Joy Foster for encouraging me to include the story of Zak even before its happy ending. Major shout out to my editorial goddess, Marissa Colon-Margolies.

I am grateful that I can call you all friends. You went above and beyond in helping me deliver this book. You helped ensure that the manuscript was accurate—but more significantly, you ensured the message stayed true to who I am.

Thank you to Dr. Jan Teller from the Dystonia Medical Research Foundation (DMRF) and Dr. Nutan Sharma from Massachusetts General Hospital for reviewing the technical bits and having the commitment to take on dystonia with a scientific but genuinely human touch.

To some of the smartest people I ever met and consulted with about the exciting new frontiers of neuroplasticity: Rose Schnabel, Dr. Robert Chen at the University of Toronto, Professor John Rothwell at University College London, Dr. Aparna Wagle Shukla at University Of Florida, Dr. Mark Hallett at NIH, and Dr. Terrence Sanger at University of Southern California, Dr. Teresa Jacobson Kimberley at the University of Minnesota, and Dr. Angelo Quartarone at the University of Messina in Italy—thank you for your continued work to find the answers in and about our own heads.

And as this book is dedicated to Dr. Joaquin Farias, I'd like to further recognize him as an extraordinary man who is unafraid of skepticism and convention. He is a man who gives his intellect, time and effort to help others while asking very little in return. He is making life-enabling improvements to dystonia patients and their families. His confidence is one of the most important gifts I have ever received.

# Appendix: Confidence Boosters

*These are supplementary brainstorming ideas to help complete your Personal Confidence Plan.*

### KCI #1: Mental & Physical Health

- Get a physical exam
- If you have a specific health issue, research and see a specialist
- Schedule a few sessions with a coach/psychologist/therapist
- Join a gym or other fitness club
- Schedule times in your calendar to go to the gym
- Sign up for Weight Watchers or some other healthy diet program
- Keep a food journal and/or consult with a nutritionist
- Get a Fit Bit, app or other tool to monitor your physical activity
- Find a fitness buddy who will exercise with you

### KCI #2: Education and Street Smarts

- Finish any degrees you started but haven't completed
- Enroll in an adult education or community college class
- Seek out the requirements and/or apply for an advanced degree
- Read the newspaper or other real news media regularly (online or print)
- Join a book club
- Go to a museum/opera/ballet/other art and really read about what you are experiencing (preferably before you go)
- Read or talk to an expert about something you always wanted to know more about

### KCI #3: Financial & Career Security

- Ask friends you trust for recommendations for good financial advisors
- Interview and select a financial advisor
- Create a real budget for yourself that examines income, general spending, desired purchases (i.e. vacations, luxury items, college expense, etc.) and savings
- Talk to a recruiter in your industry about your current job and pay scale
- Update your résumé yourself or hire a résumé expert to help
- Look at job listings on LinkedIn to get a sense of employer requirements
- Ask your manager for a formal review (if not scheduled already)
- Schedule time each week to network through LinkedIn or in person events
- Add your hobbies to your résumé/LinkedIn profile

### KCI #4: Pastimes & Possessions

- Schedule time in your calendar every week or month to do a hobby you enjoy
- Find a hobby buddy that you can comfortably share the hobby time with
- Identify a hobby you think you might enjoy and research online or talk to someone who does it already to understand what it might cost in terms of money and time
- Identify a possession you'd really like to have and consider ways to obtain it (i.e. rent, borrow, layaway, save for, etc.)
- Add your hobbies to your résumé/LinkedIn profile

### KCI #5: Beauty & Personal Care

- Get a manicure/pedicure/haircut/hair coloring/hair removal/massage/or any personal care treatment
- Drink more water
- Ask someone who's hair you like who cuts/colors their hair and then go get a consult from that professional
- Get a makeover—even a free one at Sephora is OK
- Hire an image consultant to go through your closet and/or give you dressing tips (make sure you like the consultant's style, price and references before hiring!)
- If you feel that you need plastic surgery or medically-assisted service, seek a consult with a licensed professional and check his or her references as well as your insurance

### KCI #6: Sleep and Think Time

- Get 7-8 hours of sleep every night. Nap if needed.
- Recognize when you are tired and conscientiously don't let it control your actions/emotions
- Schedule time to just think every day. This may simply mean while driving or in the shower. Turn off music and the phone and consider this a meeting with your mind.
- Make a list of daily/weekly to do's but prioritize and then schedule time in your calendar to tackle those priorities with realistic timeframes. Evaluate each to do with the question "what is the impact if I don't do this or I don't do it in this timeframe?"
- Hire a babysitter or even put on the TV if you need time away from kids to sleep or think
- Say "No" to anything or anyone that isn't aligned with your current priorities

### KCI #7: Faith & Protection

- Go to church/temple/other religious services weekly/monthly
- Volunteer at your church/temple to help at an event or with a committee
- Read about or talk with leaders about your (or other) religion
- Contact three new insurance companies to get their advice and proposals for personal insurance coverage (home owners/renters, umbrella, life insurance, disability, auto, etc.) – don't necessarily buy all or any, but get more educated and compare info
- Price out a home alarm system (theft, fire, safety, etc.)
- Take a martial arts or other self-defense class
- Get a dog that will bark at intrusions

### KCI #8: Human Support & Connections

- Take stock of your friends—identify ones you can count on versus ones that are convenient. Make time in your calendar to spend with "real" friends
- Research and consider joining associations or clubs in your local area.
- Volunteer at a charity/religious group/school/event
- Become a Big Sister/Big Brother, Mentor, Best Buddy, etc.
- Reach out/spend time with family members every week/month
- Research your genealogy
- Participate in events that are part of your heritage/culture

AMERICAN CONFIDENCE INSTITUTE

ACI helps high potential individuals become peak performance leaders by unlocking the power of neuroplasticity: the ability to literally change your brain to gain greater control of thoughts and behaviors.

ACI's easy-to-use information and tools combine scientific research with personal coaching techniques used by professional & Olympic athletes, elite military and C-suite executives.

- ✓ **TED-Style Talks**
- ✓ **Onsite Workshops**
- ✓ **Self-Paced Online Classes**
- ✓ **Confidence Coach Certification**
  *ICF approved, 6 CCEUs*
- ✓ **Certified Confidence Coach Referrals**

*For more information, please contact us at:*

info@AmericanConfidenceInstitute.com